KT-499-771

# The Horse Owner's Stable Handbook

## Kathy Chesters

The Crowood Press

First published in 1996 by
The Crowood Press Ltd
Ramsbury, Marlborough
Wiltshire SN8 2HR

© Kathy Chesters 1996

All rights reserved. No part of this publication may be reproduced or transmitted in any form or by any means, electronic or mechanical, including photocopy, recording, or any information storage and retrieval system, without permission in writing from the publishers.

**British Library Cataloguing in Publication Data**

A catalogue record for this book is available from the British Library.

ISBN 1 86126 012 1

Photographs by Anthony E. Reynolds LBIPP, LMPA.

Line-drawings by Rona Knowles.

Typefaces used: New Century Schoolbook.

Typeset and designed by
D & N Publishing, Ramsbury,
Wiltshire.

Printed and bound by BPC Books, Aylesbury.

**Acknowledgements**

Grateful thanks to Rossie Theobald and her staff at Newton Hall Equitation Centre, Swilland, Ipswich, who made many of the photographs possible, and to Maureen Holden, trainer/showjumper, the International League for the Protection of Horses and Horse Country Equestrian Supplies.

I am sincerely grateful to all the companies and manufacturers who kindly helped with the research for this book, and would like to thank family and friends for their continued support along the way. My grateful thanks goes also to Vanessa Britton and Toni Cadden, for their valued advice and assistance.

DE MONTFORT UNIVERSITY
LIBRARY

| Date | 12·3·97 |
| Bo/ks/m | CAT |
| Class | 636·1083 |
| Suffix | CHE |

DMU 0364624 01 2

7144

# The Horse Owner's
# Stable Handbook

# Contents

# Introduction

Many years ago, towns and countryside were full of horses, providing all the services that cars and tractors provide today. The equine industry thrived, and a wealth of information and skills were passed on to generation after generation of horsemen. Sadly, over many years much of the skill was lost, as technology took over and the traditional groom's job died out. Today there are many more one-horse owners looking after their own mounts for pleasure, and the existing grooms have less time and resources at their disposal than in previous years. As a result, many of the original methods of horse management have been updated, though some traditional practices have changed very little.

Improvements within the equestrian field are constantly being developed, together with new ideas, some of which question the 'old school' methods passed down largely unchallenged over the years. This book will be useful to any owners seeking kind and efficient methods of management; it aims to present the available options, to help the owner choose those that best suit his own horse and circumstances.

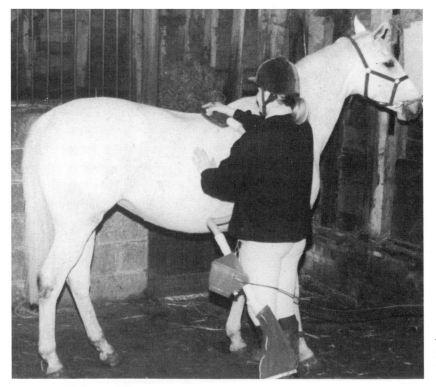

*As technology has improved, many methods of horse management have been updated.*

# 1  Understanding the Horse

Effective horse management is a goal that most strive towards but only some achieve. As all lovers of the equine will be aware, horses are exciting, unpredictable and infuriating! Therefore it is vital that we take the time to understand them, both mentally and physically. Ignorance of our horses' basic needs can be detrimental to their welfare – therefore before the practical side of stable management is addressed we must first take a look at the horse itself.

## THE HORSE AS WE KNOW HIM

There are many different types and breeds of horse and pony in the world today, each of which is suited to different climates and conditions. The horse has evolved over thousands of years and man has adapted a blend of different breeds to suit his needs. The main use of the horse nowadays is for leisure activities and hobbies, and competitive sports. The horse served a more practical purpose in previous years – as a means of transport or as a working animal – but as his role has changed over the years, so has our attitude towards him.

Today there is a horse to suit everyone, from the child's first pony to the top class eventer. With correct management and a mutual understanding, a rewarding and sympathetic relationship between horse and owner can be developed. This relationship can be very special, but it cannot be achieved unless the owner is aware of the horse's basic instincts.

*Our domesticated horses often revert to natural instincts.*

As such, the horse's psychology is important, giving us an insight into the way he thinks which can then be used to our advantage.

## NATURAL INSTINCTS

Though our modern-day horse has been domesticated for many years, he is essentially a wild animal and may revert to his instincts when stressed. It is fair to say that few horses can be trusted totally, as they are naturally highly strung and will act on impulse if scared. Whereas a human might first examine a situation and act afterwards, even an apparently calm horse can be unpredictable and take flight if alarmed.

In the wild, horses roam free, fleeing from the enemy and relying on self-preservation to stay alive. They run as herds and are gregarious creatures, and should be kept in the company of others so they do not become bored and anxious. Most herds have a hierarchy, one horse being the most dominant animal. The place of this dominant animal can be taken by the horse's owner and rider, who assumes leadership and superiority over the equine. In many cases, the horse will communicate with the owner in a way normally reserved for a mate or companion in the wild, such as nuzzling, mouthing with the lips or requesting scratches. In situations where the horse does not respect his owner and has the upper hand, the hierarchy is reversed and the horse may be uncooperative or aggressive. When he respects the herd leader and knows his place, the horse will find security living in familiar surroundings, developing habits and following rituals.

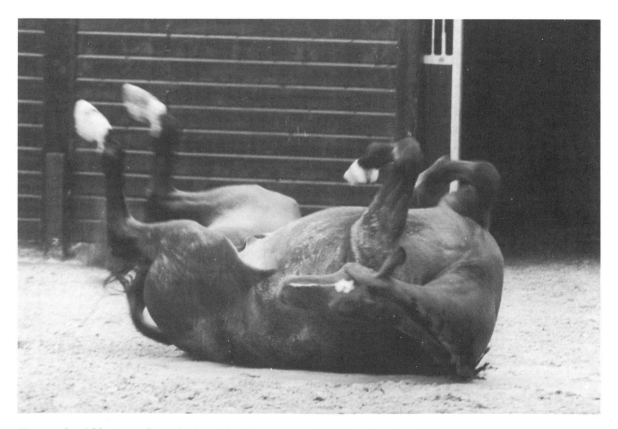

*Horses should be turned out daily so that they can undertake natural exercise.*

*If daily turn-out is impossible, alternative exercise must be given.*

## A Natural Environment

It is our duty as horse owners to make our horses' domestic situation bearable and stress-free, and this means providing as natural an environment as possible. Stabling a horse is in itself a largely unnatural thing to do, although horses' breeding and domestication by man means that many breeds as we see them today would not fare very well if kept outside permanently or released into their original wild environment. The stabled horse should ideally be turned out to grass every day, as it is essential that he gets sufficient exercise and is allowed to graze and drink at his leisure. If this is not possible or practical, for instance in a large competitive yard, each horse should be given sufficient alternative exercise daily. This could be in the form of several ridden exercise sessions, leading in-hand or working on a treadmill or horse-walker.

Horses are social animals, and feel more secure in the company of others. Where it is not possible to keep horses together, other animals may provide this company. Goats and donkeys are used as companions, and it is not unheard of for horses to befriend smaller animals such as cats, rabbits and chickens.

Just as few humans relish the idea of being restricted to a small space with very little to do, horses also need to be occupied, and may develop behavioural problems if allowed to become bored. It is interesting to note that in human society, a confined environment is given as punishment!

Horses are naturally claustrophobic creatures, and keeping them cooped up for long periods will make most horses irritable and unhappy. As the amount of time the horse spends stabled is often dictated by our busy lifestyles, it is up to every horse owner to make the experience as stress-free as possible. The stable itself should be large and well ventilated, with as much natural light as possible and plenty of warm bedding. In cold weather, horses living outdoors can run about and huddle together for warmth; when stabled they are unable to do this so we must provide the warmth for them. Most horses will be much happier if they can see other horses stabled nearby, though some will be content just to hear them.

# BREED CHARACTERISTICS

It is unwise to generalize about horses or judge their nature according to pre-conceived ideas about their breeds. A breed is just a group of horses with the same mix of original genes, and how these genes turn into individual characteristics can be influenced by various factors. Most horsey people are fans of a certain breed, their opinions possibly swayed by past experience. However, this said, each breed will have particular characteristics which may give rise to a reputation.

Generally speaking, hot-blooded animals such as Thoroughbreds and Arabs are thought to be lively and more difficult to train and manage. They are usually a lot faster and more highly strung than their cold-blooded relations, the horses suited to cooler climates such as the Irish Draught or British native pony. Through domestication and breeding by man over the years, many horses are of an uncertain origin, or are unregistered. However, the most prominent gene will usually be obvious, such as the extravagant Arab action or substantial cob build. Owing to this mixing of breeds over the years, many amalgamations of the hot blood's speed and courage, and the cold blood's temperament and conformation have resulted in versatile warm-blooded crossbreeds.

As no two horses are alike, no two Arabs should be pre-judged as scatty, or Irish Draughts lazy or clumsy. This is particularly true as everyone manages his horses differently. While certain characteristics are already in the horse's nature, they may be emphasized or lessened by correct and knowledgeable management when young.

# THE SENSES

It is easy to assume the horse's sensory organs work in the same or similar way to our own. In fact, each of the five equine senses work quite differently from ours.

## Hearing

Horses have highly developed hearing, because in order to survive in the wild they must be fully aware of danger at all times. They can hear noises above and below our own range, which is often apparent when they stand alert, listening to a sound we are not even aware of. The direction of the ear is very significant and the horse will point the tips of his ears toward the sound so he has maximum hearing. This is why it may be necessary to shout at an angry horse if you want him to take notice of you. The action of flattening the ears blocks out the sound, rather like a child covering his ears during a tantrum.

## Smell

Smell plays an important part in the horse's natural defence system. Horses living close to their original wild state, such as mountain and native ponies will use only their sense of smell to navigate new areas, to find their way back home and to locate food and water from a distance. Stallions in particular have a very well developed sense of smell, as mares in season give off strong sexual odours. All creatures send chemical messages through their own smells, called **pheromones**. When a horse can smell what he interprets as fear on a scared human, he is picking up these chemical messages.

*The Flehmen stance.*

Stallions use a stance known as *Flehmen*, where they roll their upper lip back and close the nose to trap the scent of a mare. Other horses do this in order to establish the origin of a new, unusual smell in the air. This is particularly so in the case of chemical smells, such as fly repellents or aerosols.

## Sight

There are several main differences between the seeing abilities of horses and humans. Whereas a healthy human eye is equipped with the equivalent of a zoom camera lens, focusing on objects both near and far away, the horse needs to lift or drop his head to see different objects. Coupled with a slit-shaped pupil, giving what we would consider widescreen vision, and blind-spots directly in front of the face and behind the rump, the horse needs to turn his head to look at most things. This explains their reaction to many situations for which they are often punished by humans. For instance, the horse who is approached from behind when being caught will often throw his head up in alarm and take flight. Usually he is not refusing to be caught; he just did not see the person. Also, horses that shy at objects in hedgerows have often not seen the

'foe' until they are practically on top of it, the natural reaction being one of surprise.

There are differing opinions on whether or not horses can distinguish between colours. Certainly they cannot see in the same colour vision as we can, though research suggests that some horses can differentiate between certain colours within the spectrum. Shades and textures are seen, and the daylight or artificial light available influences how the object looks. For example, a white showjump may seem quite harmless until bright sunlight lands on it, and the darkened corner of a trailer is much less daunting with a light on or a door open.

## Touch

Touch is an important form of communication for horses. They find food on the ground and test the feel of something before touching it properly (for instance, a new fence or fresh snow on the ground) using the sensors on the end of their whiskers.. Therefore, it is unkind to cut or trim the whiskers for cosmetic reasons. Horses use touch when playing or grooming their equine friends or when expressing affection, whether it be to humans or other horses.

The horse's body is very touch-sensitive, to varying degrees and in different places. This is apparent in the sensitive horse who finds grooming and clipping ticklish.

## Taste

Taste and smell are quite closely linked. Most horses, due to their biological programming, consume their food quickly, smelling as they go, without stopping to try to savour every mouthful. A horse is more likely at first to spit out something foul tasting than refuse to eat it, though some finicky horses may be quite choosy about what they consume. Horses enjoy sweet-tasting food like carrots and sugar, so succulents such as these can be fed to encourage fussy eaters. The majority of horses avoid bitter-tasting food, which is fortunate as most poisonous plants taste unpleasant and are therefore usually avoided by the horse. However, medicines are often bitter, and may have to be disguised with pleasant tastes to avoid them being left in the bottom of the feed bowl!

# BODY LANGUAGE

Though some people unfamiliar with horses' characteristics may think they are inexpressive creatures, much can be learned from their body language and expressions. As we get to know our horses, we gradually get to know their physical and verbal signs, too. For instance, when a horse is angry or bad tempered, he will put his ears back and wrinkle the nostrils. If this is accompanied by an outstretched neck and bared teeth, you can be pretty sure he is threatening to bite! The same expression with the horse's rear end facing you means he is threatening to kick. With some animals this may indeed only be a threat, though you should never give them the benefit of the doubt.

As anyone who rides a skittish horse will know, seemingly insignificant objects can scare a horse terribly. In this instance, the facial expression will change dramatically, with the ears pricked, the nostrils flared and the eyes wide.

Once a relationship has been established between owner and horse, both will start to recognize certain signs. For instance, horses will pick up the body language of a tense and nervous handler, feeling the jerky movements and sensing fear. This is why it is essential to be calm and relaxed around horses, always using slow limb movements and speaking in a relaxed manner. This will also prove beneficial when chastisement is necessary, as the horse will recognize the change in the tone of voice when it is raised or when words are spoken more firmly.

Though we feel that our horses understand what we say most of the time, it is fair to say that they only recognize certain words and phrases, those that are repeated over and over again. For instance, the horse's name, or phrases used regularly such as a gentle 'Whoa', a sharp 'No' or a praising 'Good boy'. As the horse learns to recognize these sounds and is praised when he does so, he will associate his movements with the sound the word makes. He is not learning the meaning of the word, nor the word itself. This is why when training a horse the phrases should all sound very different so as not to confuse him.

A reassuring voice is always useful when trying to calm an excited or scared horse. Irritable, loud owners often unwittingly create excitable horses, through shouting and making the horse nervous. By the same token, laid-back owners often have calm and docile horses, giving natural relaxed body signals to their animals.

# HANDLING

Bearing in mind the horse's natural instincts and state of mind, it is essential that owners handle their horses appropriately from the start. Many behavioural problems and vices are brought about by bad handling when the horse is young. This could be down to the owner's inexperience, or impatience and lack of tolerance for a young horse.

It is essential always to move quietly around the horse, as fast unexpected movements can cause nervousness and apprehension. Too much arm waving and shrieking when teaching a youngster may result in a permanently head shy horse, so the owner should speak quietly and confidently in order to earn the horse's trust. Once a relationship has been established, the horse will recognize different tones of voice, and will be able to differentiate between encouragement, praise and chastisement.

It is important that the owner physically handles the horse with affectionate contact such as stroking, grooming and patting. A horse that is not afraid of his owner's touch will be more co-operative in general, and will be easier to manage when introducing new practices such as clipping or wearing new rugs. Most horses are ticklish in areas where the skin is at its thinnest, such as around the sheath or between the forelegs, so the owner should get the horse used to being touched all over the body.

It is always best to be cautious when handling horses, and safety must always be paramount. A horse that is approached directly in front may bring his head up in alarm, hitting the handler in the face. Then there is always the risk of getting kicked when approaching from directly behind the horse. Though owners invariably trust their animals once a bond has developed, it is never safe to do this totally. Horses are essentially unpredictable animals. The shoulder is generally regarded the safest place at which to approach a horse, especially when he is loose or unaware of the person's presence. When approaching from a distance, it is always best to announce your presence verbally to avoid alarming him.

A confident manner when handling horses will serve to reassure. Horses are sensitive to emotions and can tell when someone is nervous or scared. This, combined with an authoritative tone, is the basis of effective handling. The horse will learn to respect the owner and recognize commands through tone of voice and body language.

A policy of reward and punishment is also useful in order to establish a good working relationship with the horse, though both should be appropriately administered in order to be beneficial. Praise will go such a long way, and can come in many forms. Even if the horse has moved over a step or lifted a foot up when requested, a kind word or a pat will soon let him know that he has done well. When used consistently, these praises can form a vital part of the handling programme, as horses are generally co-operative animals and will be

*Handling is important and earns the horse's trust.*

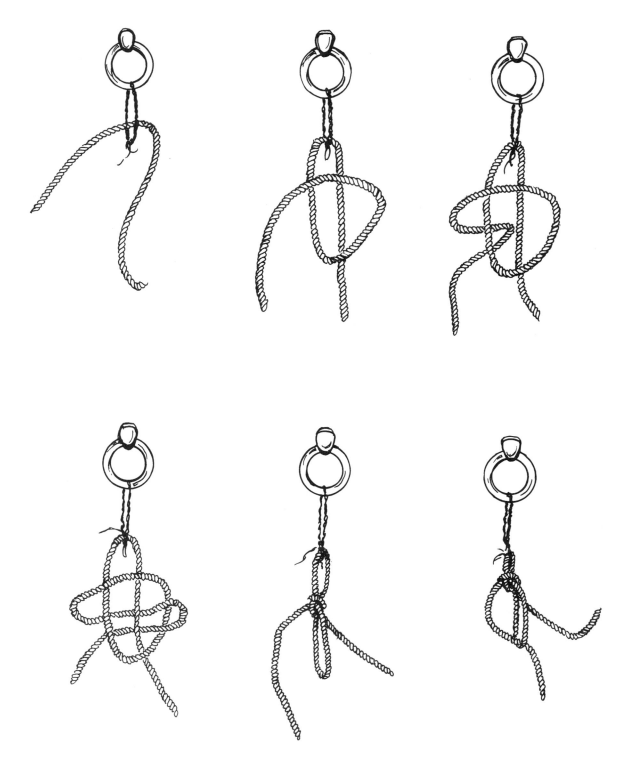

*Tying the quick release knot.*

grateful for a little encouragement. Edible rewards are certainly useful for certain occasions, but can create behavioural problems such as biting if given too often. These rewards may prove useful when overcoming fear, such as teaching a horse to load into a trailer or horsebox. Often the thought of food at the other end of the box can over-ride the fear of the unknown, as horses will rarely turn down a tasty treat.

Punishment is often given out inappropriately, sometimes when the handler is at fault or just plain bad tempered. This kind of behaviour is often witnessed at shows when tired and frustrated owners take out their anger on a confused horse. Punishment should be administered only when it is deserved, and it must be immediate.

Leading the horse should always be done correctly. Never wrap the rope around the hand, or drag the horse from in front. He should be encouraged from the leader's position by the shoulder. The rope should be held in both hands, and the horse turned away from the leader to prevent his being trodden on. It is best to avoid the rear end of a horse as even the most trustworthy animal can kick unexpectedly. If it is necessary to go behind the horse, it is safer to keep close to him as a kick from a distance will have more force. Most horses give warning signs if they are about to kick, but not if they feel threatened

*Some disobedience puts the handler at risk.*

or are genuinely nasty. In this case it is sensible to avoid the rear end altogether!

The safety of the handler is also important. Always wear sensible sturdy shoes or boots, and gloves when leading horses. A riding hat should be worn when handling young horses or unfamiliar horses in unfamiliar situations. As all horse owners should know, even the smallest task, such as loading or clipping, can be dangerous where unpredictable animals are concerned. As such it is advisable to wear protective headgear at all times, although it is up to individual handlers to protect their heads at their own discretion.

## BUILDING A RELATIONSHIP

The key to obtaining a rewarding relationship between horse and owner is to treat the horse as an individual, and with respect. It is certainly easier to build up a good relationship if the horse has been owned by the same person since he was young. When a horse is bought after he has been schooled and trained, he will have learned to trust someone else and to recognize their commands. Getting to know a new horse requires a lot of time and patience.

A horse that respects his owner does not fear him. The horse will learn to respect through trust, familiar, reassuring surroundings and regularity. A timid and frightened horse, especially a youngster, may take a long while to realize this new owner and potential leader is not a threat. Just spending time in the field or stable talking to the horse and reassuring him can be the basis of a strong relationship. There is a bonding and training technique, introduced by the American Monty Roberts, which successfully demonstrates the trust and willingness most horses are prepared to give. It works on the principle of gaining the horse's trust when training, and using his natural willingness and disposition to an advantage.

Once the initial bond has been established, it is important to instill discipline. A horse with no manners is usually an unpleasant horse to own. Discipline plays an important part in horse management, and is all about respect. Most horses are natural followers, and find security in human leadership. It is a sad fact that some owners take advantage of this fact, trying to push their animals into submission by brute force or aggression. This is taking advantage of the natural good nature and willingness of most horses. First of all, basic consistent rules should be taught and the horse will need to adhere to these daily. For instance, walking on when asked, standing quietly, picking his feet up, and moving over in the stable when requested. These and other basic procedures are relatively easy for the horse to understand if taught by association of ideas and with praise given when appropriate. Once simple tasks have been learnt, the same principles can be used to teach other things, including ridden work.

Titbits can prove useful when disciplining horses, as food is the one thought uppermost in their minds. This is not greediness, but a biological need to survive. While a sweet or carrot can serve as an extra treat for good behaviour, excessive feeding of titbits can lead to nipping and bad manners, and should be carefully monitored. It is usually more effective to give a pat and a verbal 'Good boy' than a titbit.

Everyone has different ideas on disciplining horses with regard to chastisement, and the amount given can often depend on the horse in question. A sharp 'No' may often suffice for a small misdemeanour such as fidgeting, but a smack may be necessary for defiance or nastiness. The size and strength of horses (and indeed of the smallest pony!) means that some disobedience is simply not acceptable, especially if it puts the handler at risk. For example, a playful nip when grooming a ticklish spot can be tolerated, but a vicious kick or bite deserves an immediate smack along with a cross word. The horse will soon learn not to do it again. It is very important that the chastisement is given immediately so the horse relates it to what he has just done. If the owner quietly seethes for ten minutes before telling his horse off, the deed will have been forgotten, and the owner will be starting a vicious circle of defensive biting or kicking caused by the horse's confusion and fear.

The majority of horses are quite willing to co-operate and respect their handlers. However some horses, particularly if they have been subjected to bad management, may need a little extra telling off. This should never amount to losing your temper or using unnecessary force, and ultimately should be left to an experienced person's discretion. Anyone who encounters behavioural problems with their horse that they can't handle should seek knowledgeable help, as one wrong move when disciplining can lead to many problems later on.

## VICES

Vices are behavioural problems which are generally brought about by bad management, combined with boredom. They are notoriously difficult to cure, so prevention is always the best measure. Some stable vices may be picked up and copied from another horse; this often happens in the bigger yards where there are lots of bored horses!

There are steps that can be taken to prevent the vices occurring. The first is to alleviate boredom. Providing regular exercise routines, including suitable turnout programmes, will go a long way to prevent monotony. A horse confined to the stable for long periods of time will need to get out and relax in the field, or have a change of scenery in order to get rid of pent-up energy. The stabled horse should also have constant access to hay. If the holes in the haynet are quite small, it will be more difficult to eat, and will keep the horse occupied for longer. Company is another important factor in preventing boredom. Even if the horses are not close but can actually see one another this will serve to reassure them and reduce anxiety.

### Box-walking

The horse that paces around his box is usually nervous, and consequently should be kept in an environment with the minimum amount of stress. His problem could have originated from getting cast in the stable, so plenty of clean bedding should be provided with comfortable banks to lessen the chances of this happening again.

Horses like to play and may be grateful of a new game in the stables. Footballs, either left on the floor to be kicked around or hung up within a net to be nudged, are given by some horse owners to occupy their animals. The same principle can be applied when horses are turned out, especially if there is limited space in the field or little grazing. Large resilient balls are now available for horses to play with, and can be picked up or kicked around. They are very useful for mischievous youngsters who get bored easily.

### Weaving

Another anxiety-related stable vice is weaving, where the horse swings his head and forelegs from side to side. His whole front half may sway, with the feet lifting up or stamping the ground. This is a serious vice, as it can progress from a nervous habit in to an addiction.

A weaver is classed as unsound, therefore losing value and in some cases becoming a liability. As weaving is easily picked up and copied by other horses in close contact, most livery yards will not accept a horse with this habit. The best method of prevention is to give a stress-free, organized lifestyle, with regular exercise, turn-out and feeding times. Feeds should be given promptly, as the excitement of waiting can cause the horse to weave in anticipation. Weaving grilles can also be fitted on to stable doors, although these have only limited success: a confirmed weaver may step back from the grille and continue to indulge in the habit.

## Windsucking and Crib-biting

Crib-biting is a serious vice which can impair the digestive process.

Windsucking and crib-biting are two similar, serious vices involving the swallowing of air. When the horse crib-bites, he holds an object such as a fence or door with his teeth, and gulps loudly. A windsucker gulps air in a similar manner, but does not need to hold on to an object and, as the name suggests, just arches his neck and swallows. These vices can impair the digestive process, and lead to excessive amounts of air in the digestive tracts, causing colic or flatulence.

Windsucking collars prevent air being sucked down by stopping the throat muscles contracting. Crib-biting buckets can be fitted around the muzzle for a short-term cure, but these can hamper grazing. Should the horse attempt to drink it could be dangerous, as the water could go up the nasal passage. Removing any objects that the horse can grab hold of, or covering them with an anti-chew substance or a piece of thick plastic drainpipe may help. However, as with most vices, once established they are difficult to cure; regular exercise, turn-out and feeding programmes (including unlimited hay) are the best methods of prevention.

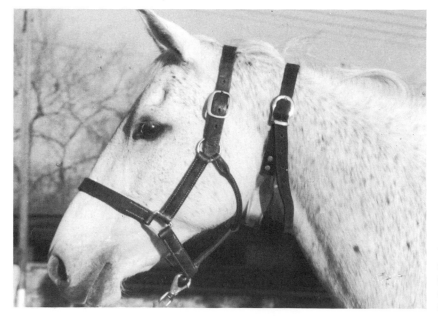

Windsucking collars stop the throat muscles from contracting, thus preventing the horse from gulping down air.

A horse with a vice is not necessarily a bad horse. His habits may have been brought upon by careless management. Whether or not you choose to buy or keep a horse with a vice largely depends on your requirements. For instance, someone who wishes to compete will reduce their chances of success and maybe harm the horse if he has damaged wind due to long-term windsucking. However, if the horse's good points overshadow a small vice causing little harm, you may feel he is worth persisting with. By creating a pleasant and stress-free environment, the owner of the horse with a long-term vice is doing the utmost to alleviate the problem. However, once the habit has occurred it may be impossible to cure.

# CONFORMATION

What you look for in a horse's conformation should directly relate to his use or purpose.

For instance, a large cob with a strong neck would probably not suit a competitive child, and a lightweight pony may not fare well in the hunting field. Though all breeds differ in their physical make-up, there are certain aspects of good and bad conformation that always apply. Some may argue that good riding conformation is not that important for a family pony, companion or pet. However, most conformational defects can lead to weaknesses in any horse, whatever their use.

## Head and Neck

The horse's head and neck should be well proportioned with each other, and with the rest of the body. If the head is heavy, its size could affect the horse's balance, and ultimately his way of going. If the horse is to excel at physical work he will need large, well-rounded nostrils to ensure the maximum intake of air. Well-spaced the jawbones will allow flexion at

*Good conformation is important, and should be assessed in relation to the purpose for which the horse is kept.*

the poll, and a set of even, well-set teeth should see the minimum of bitting problems. An overshot jaw is known as a parrot mouth, and apart from looking unsightly in some cases, it can also lead to difficulty in eating and digesting food properly. The crest of the neck should be longer and more 'developed' than the underside. A ewe neck, in which the underside muscles are well developed and the upper ones weak, appears 'upside down'; this type of neck causes the horse in work to become very heavy on the forehand and unable to flex his neck properly.

## Withers

As a rough guide, the withers of a mature horse should be level with the croup, the highest point of the quarters. As a young horse develops, both points will overtake each other, and at maturity their level should be similar. This is not to say that a horse with high withers will not perform well, but shoulder muscles may be weaker and more susceptible to strain and injury. Balance and tack-fitting problems may occur, and perhaps lead to back problems. Flat withers often accompany straight shoulders and a short, choppy action.

## Shoulders and Chest

The conformation of the shoulder is usually linked to that of the withers. A long and sloping shoulder is ideal, providing a more economical movement; that is an easier and more comfortable action. The chest should be spacious enough to provide plenty of lung room, but not so wide that a rocking movement is produced when the horse is exercised. A narrow chest can lead to a stilted stride and brushing, that is where the lower part of the legs knock or brush together.

## Back and Quarters

The horse's back needs to be strong, as a weak back, even in an unridden horse, can lead to

problems with the limbs and overall action. The back should have a slight natural dip; a hollow or swayed back can cause difficulties in engaging the hindquarters. The opposite, a roach back, encourages a choppy action and gives an uncomfortable ride. Both can lead to tack-fitting problems. The quarters should be well defined and muscled, as they provide most of the power and impulsion. The croup should be at a similar level to the withers, though if slightly higher with a defined bump is said to be the sign of a good jumping horse.

## Limbs

The forelegs should have prominent flat knees, fairly upright pasterns and above all strong, straight bones. There are several conformational defects in the forelegs that can lead to problems: *over at the knee*, where the knee bends slightly forward; *back at the knee*, where the lower limb has an inward curve, and *tied in below the knee,* where the circumference of the lower part of the knee joint is small and the bone is weak. Everyday stress and concussion on the forelegs can create weaknesses that can lead to unsoundness and injuries.

The hind legs assist with and the quarters create the impulsion and, as with the forelegs, must be strong and straight. The hocks need to be large so they can flex and provide power, and the pasterns should not be too long or sloping. Conformational defects in the hind legs include *cow hocks*, where the hocks turn inward making the legs appear bowed, and *sickle hocks,* where the joint is over bent, making the leg from stifle to fetlock take on the shape of a sickle.

## Feet

The horse's feet are extremely important: as the saying goes, 'No feet, no horse'. The feet should be matching pairs, as differences in the size or angle can affect the horse's action. The majority of farriers agree that fairly upright feet (as opposed to wide and flat) are most desirable, that is at an angle of approximately 50 degrees to the ground. The heels should be open, the frogs in contact with the ground and the soles strong. The subject of the horse's feet is an extensive one and any queries or problems should ideally be discussed with a farrier. Unfortunately, the majority of horses with badly conformed feet are likely to have poor action and additional problems or weaknesses.

# KNOWING YOUR HORSE

The horse is an individual, from his mental capacity and temperament to his pain threshold and susceptibility to illness. Once the owner can recognize what is normal for his horse, it is much easier to diagnose his pain or discomfort, rather than relying on a textbook of symptoms that your horse may not display. Even the knowledge of small things, such as aversions to types of feed or even clothing, may come in useful if your horse is off colour. To illustrate this point, one horse I know is scared stiff of wearing back leg straps on New Zealand rugs, as a result of a traumatic experience he encountered when young. If an unsuspecting person should turn him out in such a rug, he walks jerkily with his legs underneath him, looking for all the world as if he is severely lame in both hind legs. It is, however, very important to know the basic signs of good health so diagnosis of illness will be made much easier.

## Signs of Good Health

- The horse should have a general sense of well-being about him. That is to say, he should be alert and interested in his surroundings, with his head up and ears pricked. He should have good posture and not be resting any limbs, though it is not unusual to rest a hind leg when dozing or totally relaxed. Resting a foreleg is more cause for concern.

- The eyes should be bright, with a clear surface and no discharge. The mucous membranes beneath the eyelids should be a salmon-pink colour.
- The horse's skin should be loose and supple, with a sheen on the surface and no excess scurf or dirt underneath the hairs. It should also lie flat, though wearing turnout rugs in the winter can ruffle the coat. When the skin is gently pinched between two fingers for a few seconds before releasing, its natural elasticity should allow it to lie flat immediately afterwards. In an older horse the skin will take longer to do this, and doesn't necessarily mean he is in bad condition for his age.
- The droppings should be regular with a moist consistency, and upon hitting the ground should break. The average horse passes around ten droppings a day, though this depends on the diet, the amount being fed and the size of the horse. The passing of urine should again be regular, and almost colourless with no strong or offensive smell.
- The teeth should be even and flat with no sharp edges, and the gums and inner lips a salmon-pink colour.
- The average horse's temperature is 100–100.1°F (37–38°C). This will vary according to the work the horse has been doing, so it is important that he has time to recover after exercise before taking the temperature. However, a temperature that is higher or lower than normal, without there being an obvious reason, may indicate illness.

## Taking the Horse's Temperature

The horse's usual temperature is 100–100.1°F (37–38°C). There are two kinds of thermometer available: the traditional mercury type made of glass and encased in plastic, or the plastic battery-powered digital ones. Both are effective, but the digital thermometers, though a little more expensive, are slightly more accurate and easier to read, and probably safer to have around the yard as they contain no glass and will not leak mercury. Both

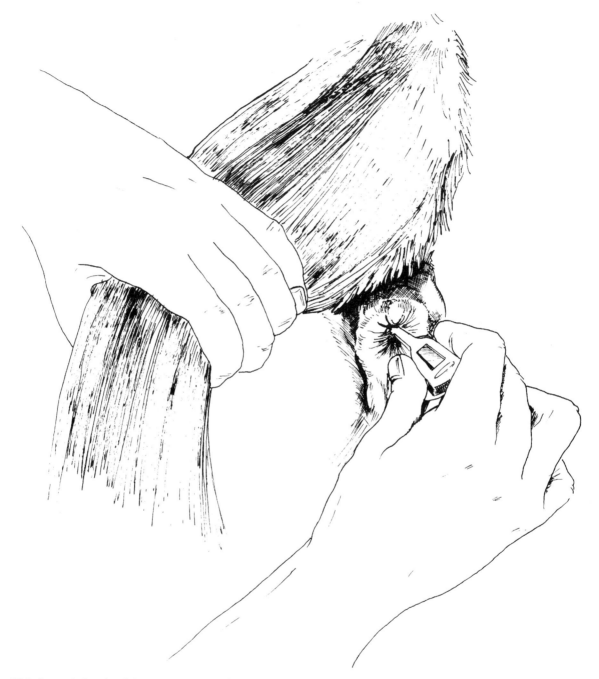

*This horse is having his temperature taken correctly with a digital thermometer.*

kinds are available from most saddlers, tack shops or veterinary surgeries.

Although some horses may be apprehensive at first, taking the temperature is painless and they soon get used to it. Proceed as follows:

1. Tie the horse or have him held held by an assistant if he is unaccustomed to the procedure.
2. Grease the thermometer with a little petroleum jelly.
3. Lift the tail and, with a rotating action, insert the thermometer into the rectum. (It is not unusual for the muscles in the rectum to draw the thermometer inwards, so it should be held firmly.)
4. Hold the thermometer in place for approximately one minute, then remove it gently. Read the temperature and wipe the thermometer clean.

## Taking the Horse's Pulse

• The average horse's pulse rate is between thirty-six and forty-two beats per minute. These figures vary between horses, with some highly strung animals having naturally higher pulse rates. The usual recovery time after exercise for the pulse to return to normal is fifteen minutes.

The usual places to take the horse's pulse are under the jawbone, above the eye at the temple, or on the inside of the foreleg level with the elbow. The pulse should be taken with the first two fingers, pressing quite firmly and counting for thirty seconds. Double the figure to get the amount of beats per minute.

## Taking the Horse's Respiration

• The average horse's respiration rate is eight to fifteen breaths per minute, one inhalation and one exhalation counting as one breath.

Standing either behind or to one side of the horse, watch the amount of times the horse's sides rise and fall per minute. This can be very difficult, especially in a very fit horse. It is easiest to take the respiration rate while concentrating on the area of the flank known as the heave line, which is approximately five inches (12.5cm) above the belly line between the elbow and the stifle. The respiration rate should be taken both after exercise and while at rest. This will enable you to develop an understanding of what is 'normal' for your horse.

## Keeping a Record

It is always a good idea to keep a record of your horse's details in a logbook, which should be kept in an accessible place in the vicinity of the stable yard. This should include average temperature, pulse and respiration at rest (TPR) and details of general health. Though some details may seem insignificant, such as the temperament and habits of the horse, or how many droppings he does every day, these details will save time should someone else have to administer veterinary help in the owner's absence. Relevant allergies, previous illnesses and treatments and veterinary contact numbers should also be logged in the book. It will serve as a reference point in the future, and in an emergency situation could prove invaluable. Horses may react differently or strangely when ill, so if their reactions can be identified as 'normal' or 'abnormal' their diagnosis will be quicker.

---

ECONOMIZE

• Instead of spending money on expensive toys for bored horses with vices, owners could put resilient footballs inside haynets hung above the stable door. This will help to keep the horse occupied.
• Time and money may be saved in the long run if you keep a record of your horse's details in a logbook. If for any reason the veterinary surgeon requires information regarding the horse, the details will all be accessible and diagnosis may be quicker.

# 2 Stabling and Pasture

## KEEPING THE HORSE AT LIVERY

There are several different ways of keeping horses, each one differing according to the owner's requirements and financial circumstances. For the majority of one-horse owners who hold down a full-time job and/or run a family, the most popular method of horse-keeping is at livery.

The three main forms of livery are full, working and DIY. However, there are many establishments that offer special combined livery deals. When approaching different yards, it is always best to find out exactly what services are available, and even what you as the horse-owner can offer the yard. As the livery cost can vary dramatically, it is advisable to shop around until an establishment has been found that suits everyone concerned, especially the horse.

### Full Livery

When paying for full livery, the horse owner should expect all the hard work to be done for them, including mucking out, turning out and feeding. Depending on individual yards and the amount of livery money being paid, additional work such as grooming and exercising may be undertaken, too. Full livery is available at a variety of places, from the local riding school or farm to competition yards and BHS examination centres. The cost varies

*Facilities such as an indoor school may be an important consideration when choosing a yard.*

*The hard work is usually done for owners when their horses are at full livery.*

enormously from place to place and usually relates to the facilities available and the general standard of the yard.

## Working Livery

Working livery is offered at many riding schools. It involves a much reduced livery cost, with the hard work still being done in return for the use of the horse in riding lessons. This can be very practical, providing a strict agreement is made with regard to the amount of hours and the standard of rider the horse is used for. Because riding schools are busiest at weekends, which is also the time most owners wish to ride, this method can prove inconvenient.

## DIY Livery

This is where rent is paid just for the use of a stable and access to a field, and the owner is responsible for all the feeding, exercising, and day-to-day care and management of the horse. As well as being the cheapest form of livery – and thus very popular – it has an added benefit in that the necessary daily contact will enable you to build a better relationship with the horse than you might expect with one kept at full or working livery.

# KEEPING THE HORSE AT HOME

For those fortunate enough to own land and facilities, keeping the horse at home can prove the most convenient and economical method. Before making the stabling arrangements, it is important to make sure there is sufficient accompanying land. There should be at least one acre of land per horse, and ideally double that, so the grass can be rested and use of the fields alternated. As most horses prefer company, it may be necessary either to purchase or have on loan a companion for the horse, so the added field space must be taken into account.

## Stable Conversion

Assuming there is sufficient grazing, a stable conversion itself can now be considered. Many farm buildings in structurally good condition can be converted to stables very easily. A good stable size for a horse is approximately 12ft (3.6m) long, 12ft wide, and 12ft high. Ponies will be comfortable in smaller stables approximately 12ft by 10ft (3.6m by 3m) wide.

Traditionally, brick-built stables have always been regarded as the most desirable. If the pocket can stretch to brick conversions by a professional builder, it will be a good investment. They are certainly warmer and long lasting, but take time to build and are expensive.

Owners may choose pre-fabricated wooden and metal-grille stables to be erected within the building. The Loddon conversion, for example, is designed with practicality in mind, featuring various time-saving devices which make them popular in larger yards. These constructions will be very warm within another building such as a barn, and are much cheaper than brick-built alternatives. However, conversions can be done even more economically. Many American establishments keep their horses in a more open-plan barn environment, and many British owners are now following suit. The walls of American-style boxes are quite low so the horses can see and touch their neighbours but not get over the divide. Timber is the most readily available material from which to make these divisions, and can be erected with the help of an efficient handy-man or builder. Having said

this, many perfectly satisfactory divisions have been made with railway sleepers, concrete blocks or other solid alternatives. Whilst doors and fittings may be a little expensive, this DIY method of stable construction can prove very economical and perfectly adequate for the horse. The main disadvantage is that the ventilation may be poor. Large doors or windows that can be kept open are important, as an enclosed environment encourages the spread of germs and disease.

## Starting from Scratch

If there are no existing buildings available on the chosen site, it will be necessary to start from scratch and erect new ones. However it may not be this simple, as the erection of new buildings can be affected by the location of the property. If the location is in a town or village

*There must always be sufficient grazing to accompany a stable.*

that is not regarded by the authorities as a conservation area, there is nothing stopping you from putting up an ancillary building in the back garden. If the site is within a conservation area, or on land which cannot be considered a garden, the erection of new buildings is much more restricted and planning permission may be required. However, in most parts of the world including the UK, there are certain guidelines that must be adhered to. It is important that you find out from your local authority what rules apply before you embark on any construction at all.

Assuming the construction of the stable is above board and legal, the building process can begin. The site itself should be in a sheltered area, with dry foundations and good drainage. The air supply must be free flowing and clean, so the stable should not be erected too close to other buildings.

## Materials

The choice of materials used for building or converting the stable is down to individual preference, and ultimately affordability. Brick-built stables may have the edge on appearance and will be warm and long lasting, but there are other good, less expensive alternatives available.

The most reliable way of erecting quality stables from scratch is to purchase timber buildings in kit form from stable manufacturing companies. The choice can be made from a catalogue so that the horse owner can see what the finished product will look like. Then the company's workmen will erect the stables or will recommend a construction company to do so. This method will also give peace of mind, as reputable companies give some kind of long-term guarantee.

*Structurally sound farm buildings can be converted into stables.*

Stables made with wooden planks from a timber merchant are relatively cheap and practical to assemble, but this must be done by a builder with a knowledge of stable construction. Above all, stables must be warm, strong and safe. Ideally they should be securely built on a roughened concrete base with a drainage channel, and have double thickness walls to provide sufficient warmth. Whilst being economical, this type of DIY stable needs a lot of maintenance.

The use of metal to build stables is inadvisable in cold climates, as it provides little warmth and is also quite noisy. Horses who kick the door can easily get to like the sound, and the resulting attention it brings! However in warmer climates, it is more widely used.

### Roofing

**Tiles** Traditionally the most widely used roofing material, these are made from concrete, clay, slate, shingle or mineral felt. They are reasonably priced and provide a warm environment, though in storms and bad weather, clay and slate tiles damage easily if not maintained throughout the year.

**Felt** This is relatively cheap and easy to fit, keeping the stable cool in the summer and warm in colder weather. Traditional untreated felt roofs can be a fire risk, though mineralized glass fibre or glasphalt felt is now widely used as a safer alternative.

**Galvanized iron** Extremely popular, galvanized iron is economical and highly portable. Because of the insulation underneath it is warm too, though in the wind and rain it can make for a very noisy roof.

**Onduline** A strong, durable roofing material that is available in corrugated sheets made from organic fibres. As it will not rust and is inflammable, it is very popular, and available in different colours.

**Tile sheets** A combination of traditional tile and modern sheet roofing. They are available in lightweight coated steel or corrugated cement fibre. Tile sheets give the pleasing appearance of tiles, and come in a range of colours to suit the stable construction. Though initially expensive compared with the other materials, they are maintenance-free and very durable.

### Flooring

The most important features of a stable floor are good drainage, with a forward sloping floor, and with a slightly roughened surface to prevent slipping.

**Stable bricks** These provide a very good surface but are comparatively expensive. Natural chalk or clay floors are warm and non-slip, but chip and wear away very easily.

**Concrete** The cheapest flooring, although it must be roughened when wet to give a good surface. Placing an old drainpipe on the wet slab provides an excellent shape for a drainage channel, which should drain towards the front of the stable and out through a small exit hole.

**Rubber matting**. A very good alternative floor covering, it is also widely used as a substitute for bedding. It provides a warm, insulated surface and reduces the risk of injury, and though initially expensive is long-lasting and practical.

### Ventilation

Good ventilation is absolutely essential as the horse's body thrives on plenty of fresh air to remain fit and healthy. A stuffy environment breeds harmful dust spores and can result in coughs and colds, and in severe cases even damaged wind.

Ideally, the stable should have a top and bottom door, the top being a main inlet for air and closed only in very bad weather. The window should be either hinged on the base opening inwards, directing the air above the horse's head to the roof, or hinged at the top opening outwards. The difference in air flow is much the same using either method, but if the window opens outwards there is one less object in the stable for the horse to catch himself on. Protective bars or a metal grille should be fitted over the inner window pane to prevent breakage. Window-sized doors fitted in the rear wall of the stable create good air flow when opened, and should be fitted approximately 4ft (1.2m) from the ground so the horse can look out through them. Roof ventilators running along the ridge, or overlapping Louvre Boards in the sides near to the ridge are an excellent way of ensuring good ventilation. They should be fitted when the roof is built, but may not suit all constructions, and must not allow access for rain or draughts.

In the winter it is easy to assume the horse feels the cold as we do, and so shut his doors and windows to keep him warm. Good ventilation is just as important in cold weather, and putting an extra blanket under the night rug will be more beneficial than shutting the air inlets. Heavy duty mains-powered ionizers can be fitted in the stable, and it is claimed that they improve the quality of the air. They do not assist with ventilation but they are useful for clearing the air as they provide a stream of negative ions. They are especially useful in dusty environments, and in my opinion make the air smell much cleaner.

*Fixtures and Fittings*

Stable doors should be 4ft (1.2m) wide, to ensure the horse does not catch his hips on the sides when walking in and out, and a total of 8ft (2.4m) high. If the doors are the traditional type with a top and bottom half, the usual division is 4ft (1.2m) high for each door, though the bottom door can be slightly higher (approximately 4ft 6in – 1.4m), to ensure the horse cannot climb over. The bottom door should have a kick-bolt at the bottom and a sliding bolt at the top. As some horses can get hold of the handle and play with it or even open the door, the type with a long handle section may be the safest.

Sliding doors should have the same measurements though the top section, usually in the form of metal bars, will be fixed. The fastening section must be constantly checked as these doors can look secure when in fact they are not quite shut.

Windows should start at least 8ft (2.4m) from the floor and be protected from the inside with a grille or bars. Any hinges or attachments should lie flush and not project towards the horse.

Kicking boards are optional and not widely used by the one- or two-horse owner as they sometimes encourage habitual kicking. However they are useful as they protect the stable wall, and are fitted from the floor to approximately half-way up the walls.

Fittings should be kept to a minimum in the stable so the horse has as little as possible to knock against. Mangers are optional, depending on the type of feeding system. If the feed is tipped daily into fixed mangers inside the stable, they should be approximately 3ft (0.9m) from the ground with no protruding edges. Fixed mangers can be unhygienic as they do not air and dry properly after cleaning. All feed receptacles should be cleaned daily. Removable manger holders can be fitted in a corner, but must have no sharp edges. For practicality, some yards have swivelling or hinged mangers that are filled from outside the stable and turn inwards with the feed. These are usually fitted when the stable is built as they form part of the wall, and may pose the same problems as fixed mangers in the stable with regard to cleaning.

Automatic water drinkers can be fitted in the corner of the stable. They are efficient and require little maintenance, but as their main advantage is to save time, they may not seem worth fitting for one or two horses. If the horse is prone to kicking water containers over, securing a bucket within several tyres is the easy answer; the tyres are cheap and readily available.

Two metal rings can be fitted in the stable, one at the breast level of the horse for tying up, and one at a few inches above his eye level to hang a haynet from. A hayrack may be fitted as an alternative to a haynet, at head level so that the horse does not need to lift his head and subsequently get hayseeds and dust in his eyes.

## Facilities

Additional facilities will depend on how many horses there are and the size of the yard. The bare essentials are a shed or stable for storing hay, bedding and tools, and an additional building for equipment such as feed bins, rugs, grooming box and tack. Hay and bedding can be kept outside on palettes and covered with a water-tight tarpaulin if space is very limited, but it runs the risk of getting wet and going mouldy. However, if money and space are no object, there can be separate feed, tack and equipment rooms. This is certainly preferable as most owners accumulate so much that is not always welcome in the garage at home! If one stable is being specially assembled, it may be worth building extra buildings for storage, as at least that way they will be secure and water-tight. A concrete area for cleaning buckets and an extra stable for clipping and bathing will also prove very useful. Often companies will give discounts if they are assembling several buildings, so if it is within financial reach, these additional stables may prove an investment. There must be a gate and secure fenced area around the stable, so that in the event of the horse breaking loose or getting out of the stable, he cannot go very far. A stile over a fence or a small gap between the fence and the wall gives you access but means the gate need only be opened for the horse.

# YARD EQUIPMENT

The basic equipment required at every yard, even if it only amounts to a stable and small patch of concrete, is a broom, shovel, bedding fork, plastic skip, wheelbarrow and strong hose. Brooms of differing widths, a trolley to carry feed and a garden rake will all come in useful, as will wooden beams fitted in

*Automatic water drinkers require little maintenance.*

— SAFETY —

Safety around the yard amounts to common sense, as most accidents can be avoided with a little foresight. Regular checks should be made to ensure no objects project dangerously or have become loose. All equipment should be put away or stacked, and rubbish secured in bins rather than sacks that could flap and scare the horse. The yard gate should be kept shut at all times, and the feed store shut so in the event of a breakout the horse cannot gorge himself on food.

A length of breakable string should be placed around all tying-up rings, so if the horse should pull back it is only the string that breaks. It is preferable to have a horse loose in an enclosed yard having broken the string, than pulling in vain against a solid object and panicking himself or causing damage. The leadrope should be in good condition with a safety or quick release clip and should always be tied in a quick-release knot. Leather or synthetic chrome leather headcollars break more easily than nylon alternatives, but providing a piece of string is used when tying up, they are not a necessity for everyday use. Anti-pull leadropes with an elastic section are useful for some horses who consistently pull back, as are anti-rearing headcollars which have a section attached to the leadrope that pulls tight around the nose when taut.

*A well-maintained, tidy yard is a safe yard.*

storage areas on which to hang wet rugs. At least one fire extinguisher is essential, with buckets of sand as extra fire precautions. (*See* Chapter 9 for additional information on fire prevention.)

It is also necessary to have two first aid kits, one equine, one human. The horse's first aid kit is discussed in Chapter 6; the kit for humans should consist of:
• Plasters and surgical tape.
• Gauze and lint dressing.
• Elastic bandage.
• Scissors and tweezers.
• Antiseptic lotion.
• Eye bath.

## BEDDING

A satisfactory bed is essential for the stabled horse for several reasons. It provides warmth, prevents draughts, encourages the horse to lie down and rest his legs, and also encourages staling and the passing of urine. Horses are quite fussy about where they do this, particularly if there is a likelihood of their legs getting splashed.

The depth of the bed will depend on the mucking out system used and the type of bedding, though as a general rule if the fork comes in to contact with the floor when placed on the bed it is not deep enough. Banks of bedding should be made against the walls to prevent draughts and lessen the risk of the horse getting cast. They should not be too thick or high, just enough to aid comfort and create a warm bed.

There are various considerations to make when choosing a type of bedding for the horse. Most importantly, it should be suitable for the horse concerned. For instance an animal with a cough or damaged lungs will not suit dusty bedding. The bedding should be easy to manage and muck out; therefore owners with back problems might choose a lightweight bedding with little lifting involved. It should be easy to obtain and dispose of, so the location of the stables and the yard owner's preference may be deciding factors. The cost is also important, as many horse owners are on a budget. Prices for the same type of bedding may vary in different areas, so it is best to shop around and see which kind is most economical and has good availability.

## Straw

Straw is one of the most popular types of bedding as it is easy to obtain, warm and usually very cheap. Wheat straw is the best type as it is unpalatable to the horse (oat and barley straw are readily eaten), light and easy to use and can be sold on as compost. As the bedding is quite thick, it creates good banks, giving a draught-free environment and lessening the risk of the horse becoming cast. Disadvantages are that it can be quite dusty, aggravating existing lung problems in the horse, and may cause digestive problems if eaten. Some farmers may assist with the disposal of straw muck, using it as compost for their fields. If this is not viable, then burning the muck heap is a good option providing it is in a safe area and not left unattended for long.

## Chopped Straw

Chopped straw is available in two varieties: untreated and dust-extracted. The untreated version is often produced by farmers with access to their own cutting machines, and though it is quite dusty when initially cut, it is a very economical purchase. Dust-free chopped straw is available in bales through manufacturers, and is understandably rather more expensive. In my experience it is also a

*Straw bedding is cheap and popular, but may harbour dust.*

little slippery for both horse and owner when first put down as a bed. The main disadvantage to either type is that horses may be inclined to eat chopped straw, particularly as it resembles chaff. However, chopped straw beds are easy to manage and produce a warm, comfortable surface. They also compact well on the muck heap.

## Wood Shavings

Shavings beds are hygienic, very absorbent indeed and easy to muck out. If dust-extracted, they are very useful for horses with coughs or allergies. They make an excellent deep litter bed and are also warm and comfortable for the horse.

Disadvantages include difficult muck disposal due to the slow rotting process. The bales are also cumbersome to move around and a little more expensive than the other types of baled bedding. Sawdust is similar to shavings but naturally a lot dustier. If not managed properly it ferments and becomes hot, so it is not widely recommended as an effective bedding.

## Paper

Paper bedding, which is entirely dust-free and very hygienic, is most commonly sold in bales of shredded newspaper. It provides a thick, warm bed for the horse, and in newspaper form is light and is relatively easy to muck out. On the downside, newspaper is expensive, not very absorbent and messy to use in windy weather. In certain areas it may be available from printing or office companies in small quantities. While this may be a cheaper alternative, it is even less absorbent than newspaper and is heavy to muck out. Disposal also poses a problem, though if bought in large baled quantities, it can be recycled by the manufacturers.

## Auboise

Auboise is a bedding derived from the core of the hemp plant. It is dust free and highly absorbent. It is sold in bagged or baled form under different trade names and offers a soft, comfortable bed that generates a lot of warmth. Its high absorbency levels make

*Dust-extracted shavings are hygienic, and useful for horses with allergies or lung damage.*

auboise a useful bed for deep littering, and it is easy to dispose of as it is completely bio-degradable. Disadvantages are that it is quite expensive, and due to its organic growth may be quite hard to get hold of in certain less rural areas.

## Rubber Matting

Rubber matting has grown increasingly popular as a stable bedding, being previously used as floor coverings in trailers and horse boxes. It eliminates or reduces the use of baled bedding, as once the mats are fitted in the stable only a small amount of bedding is required. Some manufacturers suggest no bedding is necessary at all, and indeed the mats can be springy and comfortable for the horse, eliminating draughts if they are fitted correctly. The surface is non-slip, and extremely durable, and most companies guarantee the product for between five and ten years. Matting available for the walls is an excellent way of preventing the horse getting cast as it has a roughened surface. It is also cushioned, and makes the stable considerably warmer. The disadvantages include the initial cost which is approximately the same as an eighteen-month supply of shavings, and the bare look of the stable, which to fans of thick beds will look cold and uncomfortable. Of course this will depend on the amount of additional bedding used, as will the appearance of the horse should he lie in his own droppings.

## Peat Moss

Generally speaking, peat moss is not commonly used, though in the rural areas where it is readily available it is a popular and cheap form of bedding for animals. It is economical and absorbent, rotting down well and giving a hygienic environment if correctly managed. Disadvantages include its unpleasantness to muck out, difficulty in distinguishing the soiled areas from the clean, and its cumbersome weight.

## Recyclable Bedding

A recyclable bedding is in the experimental stages, involving small worm-like strips of rubber. Once soiled they are put in to a machine that filters waste and cleans the bedding. The system is currently extremely expensive and seems practical only for large yards.

# MUCKING OUT

There are two main management systems of the horse's stable: daily cleaning out and deep littering. The owner's choice will depend on individual factors such as the cleanliness of the horse and the time the owner has available daily for mucking out.

## Daily Cleaning Out

This is perhaps the preferred method of the two as it is more hygienic, preventing fungal build-up and foot disease caused by ill-managed deep-litter beds.

Having removed the horse from the stable (it is usually most convenient to muck out when he is in the field) and taken out buckets and haynets, the mucking-out equipment should be assembled outside. A fork relevant to the type of bedding being used, a shovel, broom, wheelbarrow and pair of rubber gloves are the essentials.

Initially, the droppings should be removed with the fork or rubber gloves, and the wet bedding taken out. As it is being separated, the dry bedding should be banked up against the wall or stacked in a corner. Damp shavings or auboise can be left to dry out on the top of the banks if only slightly soiled, though paper and straw, once wet, should be discarded. The banks should be taken down and shaken out at least twice a week, as the compacted bedding can start to grow fungal spores if not properly cleaned. If the new bedding is used to create a different bank each time it is added, this will ensure the bed stays clean and fresh. If it is possible to leave the bedding up so the floor can air for a few hours, this will help to create a hygienic atmosphere. If this is not practical on a daily basis, the floor should be aired at least once a week. Deodorizing powder can be sprinkled on the floor to lessen ammonia smells and keep it fresh.

Mucking out rubber matting stables is a quick and easy affair. If no bedding is used, they simply need to be brushed out daily. Some types of matting are flush to the stable floor, so no moisture seeps under the mat. They can be lifted and aired a few times a year, and need minimal maintenance. Mats which are slightly raised or have grooved undersides, require a hose down every so often.

## Deep Littering

Using the deep-litter system provides a warm, comfortable bed and an efficient labour-saving system. However, it must be correctly managed as dirty beds can cause rotting feet and polluted stable air. Shavings and auboise are the materials most suited to deep littering. Straw and paper often create more trouble than they are worth, effectively turning the bed into a soggy compost heap.

Initially, enough bedding is laid down to create a deep, comfortable bed with banks. The droppings are removed daily, the surface raked over and the banks shaken up. If this is not done daily in a wooden stable, the walls may begin to rot. Extra bedding is added when necessary, and sometimes the centre is dug out and replaced if it gets too dirty. Deep litter beds have traditionally been left six months to a year before the entire bed is removed and the process begins again. However, by the end of this period the beds are usually in a dreadful state and have a pungent smell. It is much better for the horse if most of the wet bedding is dug out once a month or every few weeks, and the floor is allowed to air.

A successful combination of the two mucking out methods is employed by many owners who work during the week and may be short of time. The droppings are skipped out daily and the bed raked over, and at the weekend the floor is dug out and fresh bedding added. In my opinion this is a more satisfactory deep litter method and less detrimental to the horse's welfare than traditional deep littering.

## The Muck Heap

The muck heap arrangements are very important, as badly sited or ill-managed heaps both look unsightly and create more work. If the muck-heap is to be sited at the yard, it should be near enough to the stables for convenient use and removal, but not so close that it becomes a fire risk.

One of the most satisfactory methods to remove the muck-heap is to arrange with a local farmer to take it away to use as compost. The farmers will usually accept only straw or auboise compost, as other bedding materials do not decompose well. Burning the muck is the next best option, as leaving the heap just to rot will take a long time. If the former option is chosen, the burning must be carefully supervised. Ideally, the muck should be situated within a walled area of bricks or concrete so that the wind cannot carry pieces away, risking an unintentional fire. Once a well-managed muck heap has been lit in several places it should burn down quite quickly. It is most practical to burn the muck-heap regularly, as obviously the larger it gets, the longer it will take to burn down. Large muck-heap fires are more likely to get out of hand, causing excessive smoke and a potentially dangerous situation. When the muck is taken daily to the muck-heap, it should be flattened down and tidied with a fork. A square muck-heap is not difficult to keep providing it is compacted. When it gets too high it can be made into several layers, the muck being taken to the highest level each time. The surrounding area should be raked and kept tidy otherwise it will become poached and access will prove difficult.

# TURNING OUT TO GRASS

In the past, horses were very often kept in their stables for the majority of the time, getting regular exercise through being ridden or lead out in-hand. It would appear that more people nowadays are seeing the benefits of daily turnout, for both horse and owner. The longer the horse is turned out, the closer to his natural environment he will be. He should be allowed at least several hours a day, ideally being turned out first thing in the morning and brought in to the stable in the late afternoon or when it is starting to get dark. This regime is known as the *Combined System*, and is used by the majority of one-horse owners with limited time.

Many yards with lots of horses do not have the facilities to turn out each horse all day, and certainly daily turn-out can have disadvantages. The horse's coat may lose its sheen and will understandably get quite dusty even when the horse is well clothed. There is a danger when a fit, excitable horse is turned out he will race around and cause damage to himself. For the owners whose horses are their profession or business, the risk of injury in the field may be too high, especially if the horse is worth a great deal of money. Of course protection in the way of clothing and boots is available, but it only takes one slip in the mud to lose a season's eventing or showjumping. In these environments, exercise is given in other forms, such as work on a treadmill or horsewalker. However for the majority of people,

especially those with jobs and families, daily turn-out is the best option for all concerned. In my experience, it certainly makes for happier, more relaxed horses.

## Grass Quality

A good covering of grass with minimal weeds and no poisonous plants is essential, and enough land so at least one field can be resting while another is in use. Limestone soil is a good base for a grazing paddock, as it is high in calcium which is important for strong bones, especially in the development of youngsters. Grass seed which has been formulated to provide horses with essential nutrients is readily available, though supplements can be fed to compensate for poor quality grazing if grassland management is out of the horse owner's hands. Horses will thrive on a good pasture containing plenty of herbs and moisture, though in winter months grass will not provide much nutrition as most of the goodness will have gone.

## Enclosure

Since horses are naturally inquisitive creatures, it is essential that the field fencing is solid and safe. If there is a gap or a weak spot in the fence, they will find it. Having a large field properly fenced can be a very expensive business, but it is a basic necessity. As with all equestrian equipment, there is no point saving money at the horse's expense, as inferior fencing can lead to injury or escape. A good height for a field fence is around 4ft 6in (1.4m), though this can depend on the size of horses occupying the field.

**Wooden post and rail** Generally regarded as the best type of fencing, this is durable, solid and secure. Unfortunately it doesn't come cheap but it is a good investment, because with proper maintenance it will last for years. Traditionally creosoting has been the best method of treating wooden fencing, though this needs to be done regularly

---

**FIELD SIZE**

A rough guide to sizing the horse's field is to allow at least one and a half acres (0.6 hectares) of land per horse. There should be room to run about without crashing into field companions or the fence, and enough space for horses to see each other but enjoy solitary grazing if they wish. There is nothing worse than too many horses sharing a small, sparse piece of land and fighting with each other.

*Enclosure with man
escape.*

and can prove messy to apply. An acrylic polymer coating is now available through certain manufacturers which needs only one application and still allows the wood to breathe and flex.

**Wire** Galvanized, rectangular- or diamond-mesh steel, is suitable for equine fencing. Such fences are specially manufactured to be durable and safe, and home-made barbed- or chicken-wire versions are no substitute and must never be used. In my opinion it is unnec-

essary to use any form of farm stock wire unless it is the electric type, as there are many safer alternatives available for horses at a reasonable cost.

**Polymer** The type used for racecourse barriers is a very safe form of paddock fencing. It is shock- and weather-resistant and will give rather than break when stressed. It is mainly used at studs and racing yards for ultimate turn-out safety, but it is even more expensive than wooden post and rail.

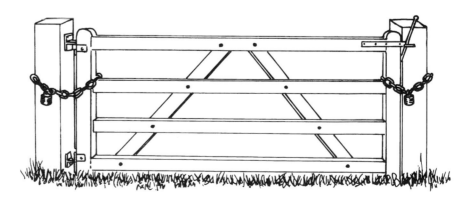

*Enclosure without man
escape.*

**Electric wire** Very useful for dividing fields, this has the advantage of being portable. However, it is advisable to have an additional fence around the boundary of the land, as it is not very strong and can be pushed over. I have seen a very determined pony sit on an electric wire fence until it collapsed so she could reach the tasty grass outside her starvation paddock!

**Electric tape** This is available in various forms and widths, and when used with wooden posts makes an economical and sound barrier. Providing it is kept taut, it is durable and strong. Combinations of wooden post and rail and tape fencing can be used to great effect. Together they have the strength and durability of wood with the deterrent properties of electric fencing. When the top rail is electrified it proves useful for preventing chewing or crib-biting.

**Flexible nylon** Bound between solid posts, this is an economical alternative to wooden rail fencing, and is quite versatile. Unfortunately it can fray and weaken after a few years, and may break under heavy strain (such as horses leaning on it to reach grass in another field).

**Existing hedges** These make good boundaries, and also provide good windbreaks. Providing they are dense, horses will not try to push through them, though an electric fence used in addition is a good safeguard just in case.

## Gates

There is little use making the fencing secure if the gates are not strong; a solid wooden or metal gate approximately 6ft (1.8m) wide is the best option. Metal can sag over a period of time if it is lent on, but is cheaper than wood. Gates should be well hung and secured properly, with a horse-proof fastening that does not project in any way. They should also have a padlock at both sides, as horse theft is made all too easy by lightweight gates that simply lift off their hinges. Some electric fencing gates are not strong or secure if used for field division, though the gate at the boundary fence surrounding the property should be substantial.

## Shelter

Some form of shelter is essential in the field, whether it be to escape from heat and flies in the summer, or from the wind and rain in the winter. Hedges and trees are excellent natural shelters, often preferred by horses to man-made constructions.

Field shelters should be erected against the prevailing wind with high roofs and plenty of space, especially if they are to be used by several horses. They should be light and airy, with good ventilation and no projecting objects. Some horses, particularly the hardy native breeds, are not keen to use their shelters in even the most unpleasant conditions. However, we should give them the option, providing a comfortable, dry area for them should they require it.

## Water Supply

A fresh supply of clean water is essential in the field, particularly if the horse is turned out for a long period of time. Automatic self-filling drinkers are very useful, especially for large numbers of horses. Though they need to be checked and cleaned out regularly, they are time saving and efficient.

Providing the field is close to the stable yard, a water trough or large container will be easy to clean out and refill with a hose. This should be done weekly, with daily checks on the water level. Metal baths are useful as they can be drained effectively, though they should be checked for rough edges. The siting for the water container is important. Drainage should be good for cleaning-out purposes, and the container should not be close to the gate as the ground will get poached and very muddy. Ideally it should be placed alongside the fence, and away from field corners and falling leaves. Natural water supplies may be suitable if the water is free-flowing, such as a small river, but they must have good access and be deep enough so the horse does not swallow silt. Ponds or other still waters are

*A large container makes a suitable field water supply, but should be checked and filled daily. This is especially important in winter when it may freeze over.*

not suitable, as the water is not fresh and may be contaminated or stagnant.

## Poisonous Plants

There are many plants and trees that are highly poisonous. Mercifully, many of them are unpleasant to taste and are avoided by most horses, but they must be removed or fenced off if they are in the vicinity of the field.

Of the poisonous plants found in pasture: Ragwort seems to be the most common while potentially lethal plants such as Buttercup, Hemlock, Ivy, and Deadly Nightshade often occur as well. There are several trees that must also never be eaten, including Yew, Rhododendron, Laburnum and Privet. Acorns and conkers can be deadly if eaten in sufficient quantities.

The speed at which some poisons attack the horse can be alarming, and there is often little that can be done to save them in serious cases. When removing plants by hand they should be pulled up by their roots, because if they break off at the stem they will probably appear again the following year.

## DAILY CHECKS AND PROCEDURES

It is important that regular checks are made on the horse and the yard facilities. Most situations may be observed during general yard duties, for instance, a loose door bolt or fraying leadrope. Each morning, when the horse is fed and turned out, he should be checked for injuries and signs of good or bad health. This is where knowing the horse's individual characteristics is important, as changes in mood or habits will be noted quickly.

Checks on equipment should also be made, such as safe leg straps and strong buckles on rugs. Feed bowls and buckets should be checked for splits and sharp edges and the stable should be inspected when mucked out for damages or loose fittings. The field fencing should be checked for broken rails or damaged sections, and the water containers should be clean and full.

When the horse is left for the night, the same checks should be made, including making sure there is sufficient hay and water and the yard gate is locked or secure. After a while this will become second nature, and will not take up much extra time. Providing the horse owner is alert and attentive, accidents can be prevented and time and money saved.

## CLOTHING

### Stable Rugs

The majority of horses in work are clipped out in the winter, and need rugs or blankets to supply the warmth their coat would provide. Even horses that are not clipped, because they are stabled and groomed, have thin coats and a lack of the natural grease to insulate their body. By giving our horses a suitable feeding plan and plenty of warm clothes, we make up for the fact that we remove their coats when they are coldest. Fortunately the selection of stable rugs available is enormous, though their prices and qualities vary.

**Cotton stable sheet** A thin sheet that can be put on as early as late summer or early autumn, when the coat is just beginning to thicken in order to keep it flat and dust-free. They provide a thin layer of warmth on their own and can be used beneath other rugs for additional warmth later in the winter.

**Quilted rug** This is the the most common winter stable rug and is usually made with a nylon outer shell, insulated or heat-reflective foil filling, and a cotton lining. They are very warm and snug, and are available in several weights suitable for different temperatures.

**Jute rug** This is cheaper than the quilted rug, and although it is not usually as warm it is available with fleece or blanket linings. Though jute has been around for many years, it has stood the test of time as it is a hard-wearing and economical fabric.

**Thermal wicking rug** This type is becoming increasingly popular as it is lightweight and versatile. They are commonly made from polypropylene, a thermoplastic material with excellent insulation and hydrophobic (non water retaining) properties. Excess body moisture is wicked to the surface of the material where it evaporates, so they are useful as stable, travelling, or sweat rugs.

**Insulux rug** Also popular, this is lightweight and contains air pockets that cool the horse in warm weather and insulate him in winter. Though useful for travelling it may not be warm enough in the stable on its own in particularly cold weather. However, when used with an over-rug its insulating properties come in to their own and the horse is kept very snug.

**Mesh sweat sheet** This is made of cotton and looks like a very large string vest. When used

*Horses clipped out in winter need stable clothing to provide them with warmth.*

40

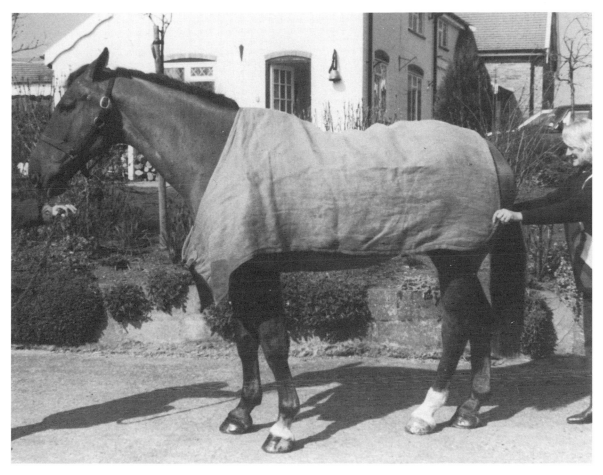

*Rugs that are too small will not give the hindquarters or belly adequate warmth.*

with a thin over-rug, they trap pockets of air between the rug and the horse's body, allowing him to dry off when wet and discouraging profuse sweating. They dry out quickly after use and are a lot cheaper than thermal wicking rugs, and very lightweight.

**Woollen, acrylic or quilted underblankets** These are used to provide an extra layer of warmth. Each equestrian clothing manufacturer seems to favour a certain synthetic material, so it is worth looking at the various brands to get the desirable weight and quality. Most are fully machine-washable too, and some can be tumble dried. This is very practi-

cal for the horse owner with little time.

Most stable rugs are fitted with surcingles or leg straps to ensure they stay in place, though some will require padded rollers or elasticated surcingles for extra peace of mind. These should not be secured too tightly as they can cause discomfort if too much pressure is put on the spine.

### Turn-out Rugs

Waterproof turn-out rugs are used to provide warmth and protection from the elements in the field.

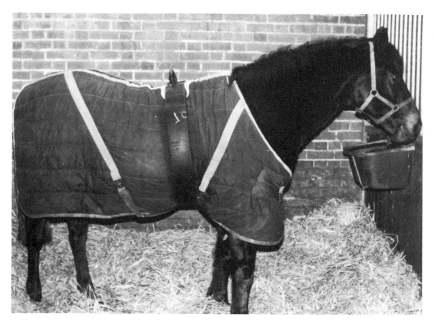

*Quilted stable rugs are popular, and available in varying weights.*

**New Zealand Rug** This is the traditional cotton-canvas rug and the most widely used. Though economical, some New Zealand rugs are not well ventilated and tend to trap moisture so they can become quite heavy when wet.

**Flax canvas** A popular alternative to cotton as the flax fibres swell when wet and mould to the shape of the horse. Flax gives a good fit and is highly waterproof, even in extreme weather conditions.

**Nylon cordura rug** A very lightweight rug made from a material that 'breathes'. It has a special hydrophilic proofing that pulls gasses away from the body to prevent condensation. Though not quite as hard wearing as the canvas rug it is very comfortable and quick drying.

*Jute stable rugs are hard-wearing and economical.*

Turn-out rugs are available in various weights for different times of year, with different linings including thermal, heat-reflective foil, and fleece. The fastenings will vary, too. Some turn-out rugs are self righting, and claim to stay in place after even the most energetic rolling session. Some have cross-over surcingles at the stomach in addition to cross-over hind leg straps, and others are very deep to give the stomach extra coverage.

Accessories for the horse include waterproof neck covers for added protection and cleanliness, and smooth undergarments that fit as chest-bibs, covering the shoulders to prevent rug chaffing.

*Fastening*
When fastening all types of rug it is safest to do up the middle section first, having fitted the rug in the correct place. This is to prevent flapping if the rug is lifted by the wind, or slipping if the horse takes fright. Hind leg straps are best left until last when the rug is secure, and should be undone first when it is removed. If the rug slips and frightens the horse with only the front end done up, he is more likely to stand still with it around his forelegs. With only the hind-leg straps fastened, he may get his legs entangled causing him to panic even more.

For the particularly thin-skinned horse, hoods and neck covers are also available for stable warmth. The hoods are usually made from lycra for a close fit to the head, though some continue down the neck and attach to the rug, and some have separate head and neck pieces. Neck covers are usually made from a corresponding material to the rug, and are extremely snug and warm.

Woollen or synthetic stable bandages provide warmth and encourage circulation to the legs. They are usually applied with padding beneath them, though are used without padding as loose 'polo' bandages by some owners. Stable bandages are commonly used when the horse is ill to secure veterinary treatments to the leg, and also for protection when travelling. Thermal wicking leg wraps are also available, and these are excellent for drying off and warming the legs after heavy exercise or bathing.

Generally speaking, the more expensive the stable clothing, the better quality it will be. Though seemingly economical, cheap canvas rugs may lose their waterproof qualities after a few years as the acids in body sweat can break down inferior quality proofing.

---

**STORAGE**

All field clothing should be stored in a dry environment when not in use, either folded in a trunk or hung from rails in a cupboard if there is enough room. This will keep the rugs well aired, as if left folded for a long while when damp they may begin to smell stale. They should be cleaned, and proofed if necessary, for the following season. Different materials will have individual washing and drying requirements, so read the manufacturer's instructions.

---

**ECONOMIZE**

- Some barn conversions are extremely costly, though successful wall divisions have been made using railway sleepers, concrete blocks or other solid alternatives.
- When preparing the first aid kits, store some items in a clean container, for instance an ice cream tub or small bucket. This can also double up as a water container used for bathing wounds.
- If choosing dust-free bedding, investigate local printing merchants who may be able to supply shredded paper at a reduced cost.
- Instead of buying a mucking-out skip from a tack shop, use an old plastic laundry basket.
- If putting a thin sheet under the stable rug to flatten the horse's coat or reduce dust, money can be saved by purchasing a bed sheet from a charity shop, rather than buying an expensive rug. By the same token, a second-hand blanket is much cheaper than an equine under-rug.
- Don't discard old, worn-out rugs as they can be used to patch up other rugs in the future, and their buckles and attachments may come in useful.
- House clearance auctions are useful places to find cheap wardrobes or trunks for equipment storage.

# 3  Routine Procedures

## WORMING

One of the most important routine procedures carried out by responsible horse owners is worming. Worms are internal parasites that can affect all horses. They cause serious damage to the horse's internal systems if not properly controlled and can in some cases cause death. Wormers are drugs that kill off the

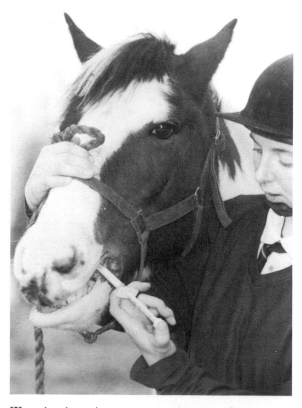

*Worming is an important routine procedure, and should be carried out every six to eight weeks.*

adult worms living in the horse's organs, and certain brands also kill off the worm larvae. It is usually through ignorance that owners do not worm their horses regularly enough, or in some unfortunate cases, at all.

All horses, ponies and donkeys should be wormed every six to eight weeks, and a record kept of the dates the drugs should be administered. As the horse's system can build up an immunity to the wormers, the brand should be changed periodically. Veterinary surgeries or stockists of wormers, such as saddlers, will advise on which type to choose and when to use it. There are various brands available in powder, granule or paste form, including herbal versions.

Although there are nine main types of internal parasites, they all have a similar life cycle. The eggs laid by mature worms within the horse's body are passed out on to the field via droppings. When a horse grazes in the field, he ingests the larvae from the droppings which have crawled on to the grass. This is why it is so important to clear fields regularly, especially if there are several horses sharing. The larvae make their way through the horse's body, settling within and living off the horse's organs, laying more eggs once they are mature. These eggs are passed out in the droppings, and so the cycle begins again.

Symptoms of a heavy worm burden within the horse include: general loss of condition, anaemia (an indication of which is pale mucous membranes under the eyelid and within the nostrils), lack of energy, recurring colic, diarrhoea, and a dropped, swollen belly. Of course each of these symptoms may point towards any number of ailments, and owners should seek veterinary advice for any medical problem they are worried about. Worm infestation rarely occurs in horses who have been owned for years by someone who worms them regularly. Worm counts can be taken by a vet to determine whether the horse currently has a heavy burden of eggs, though unfortunately the result of negligence from previous owners can materialize years later in a horse who has always appeared quite healthy.

## SHOEING AND CARE OF THE FEET

Regular attention to the horse's feet by a registered farrier is another essential practice, whether it is to shoe the horse or simply trim the feet. Poor feet do not provide good weight-bearing surfaces, as a result of which strain may be placed on other parts of his body to relieve pressure on the feet. Any horse who is regularly exercised with badly maintained feet will have limited action and could go lame.

The purpose of fitting metal shoes is to protect the feet from damage and wear from hard surfaces. As a general rule the feet will need attention every six weeks, though the regularity of the farrier's visits will depend on each horse's horn growth and the amount of work he does. For instance, hacking out every day on tarmac will wear the shoes down quickly, and visits may be necessary every month. If the work is mainly done on soft surfaces, such as fields and indoor schools, the farrier may only need to come every two months. Leaving shoes on for longer than eight weeks is unwise as the feet will have outgrown the shoes; however, if not badly worn the shoes may be re-fitted after the feet have been trimmed. Having found a reliable farrier it is best to ask his advice on the regularity of his visits. There is no point re-shoeing a horse with slow horn growth every six weeks just because it is the recommended time. The end result will be a foot with too many nail holes and an extra large farriery bill!

Though some people still take their horses to a forge, most farriers are mobile and travel to the yard. Factory-made shoes of the correct size are brought on every visit, or if they are hand-made they are prepared in advance. For speed and efficiency most shoes are factory made, and with hot shoeing can be altered slightly in the forge (a gas fire) to fit the horse's foot. Cold shoeing involves a shoe being fitted to the foot without prior heating and adjustment. This is not favoured by the majority of horse owners (myself included) as the foot is usually shaped to fit the shoe and an accurate fit is not obtained.

Even shod horses out of work and horses with no shoes need their feet trimmed regularly, again on average every six weeks. There is no law that says all horses must be shod,

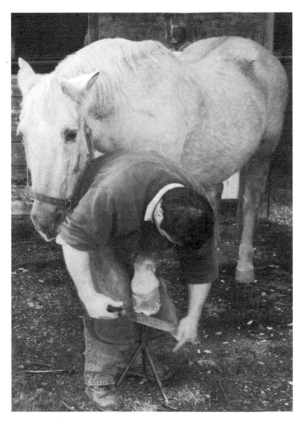

*All horses need attention to their feet from a registered farrier, on average every six weeks.*

45

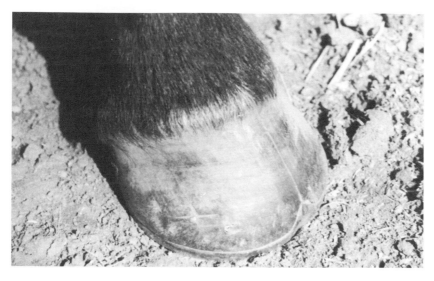

*A correctly shod foot will have good weight-bearing surfaces, and exert minimum strain on the limbs.*

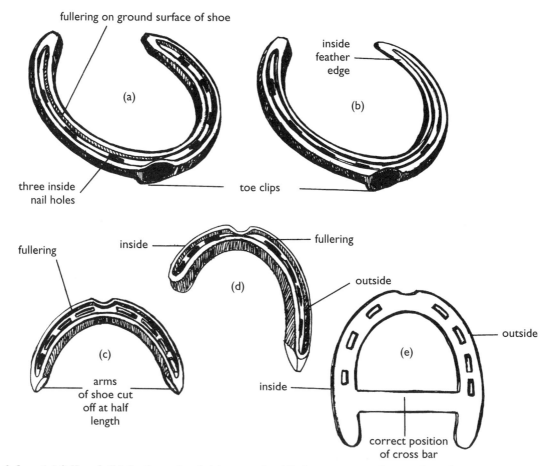

fullering on ground surface of shoe

inside feather edge

(a)

(b)

three inside nail holes

toe clips

fullering

inside

fullering

(d)

outside

(c)

outside

arms of shoe cut off at half length

inside

(e)

correct position of cross bar

*Types of shoe: (a) fullered; (b) feather-edged; (c) grass tip; (d) three-quarter shoe; (e) bar shoe.*

46

and any honest farrier will say so if he feels the horse does not require shoes. If the feet are strong and in good condition, and the horse does not work on heavy ground, he may only need regular trims.

## Types of Shoe

**Iron hunter** The most widely used shoe, this has a fullering groove on the underside to give a better hold on the ground. There are many variations including lightweight aluminium plates, plain stamped shoes with a flat ground-bearing surface, and various remedial and corrective shoes. The farrier will suggest which is most suitable having examined the horse's feet, as each horse will have different requirements.

**Synthetic lightweight** This type of shoe is glued on to the foot. They are not widely used because, while in principle they seem to be a good idea, the adhesive is not strong enough and the shoes invariably fall off within a few weeks. Currently most farriers do not recommend them, though there could well be a place in the market for synthetic shoes in the future.

**Rubber** With either aluminium or steel cores, rubber shoes are fitted with normal nails and cold-forged against an anvil. Originating in Sweden, these have yet to make an impact with British farriers.

**Boots** Though not intended as permanent replacements for shoes, they can be used for short-term exercise purposes if a shoe has come off. In my own experience I have found that by the time a horse has accepted the feel of the boot and got down to some worthy exercise, the farrier may as well have fitted a new shoe. They can cause chaffing if not properly fitted, and seem more suited for keeping foot dressings in place.

## Hoof Oils and Treatment

The use of hoof oils is a contentious issue, as while some owners choose to keep the foot supple and prevent cracking by applying it, others claim it clogs up the periople, the protective, breathable outer layer of the foot. Personally, I am inclined to agree with the latter argument. Most hoof oils are designed for cosmetic reasons and lie on the surface of the foot, sealing in little moisture, or when used in excess seep in to the horn. In my opinion, the reason so many shoes fall off is that the horn is too supple or even soggy to hold the nails in place. Truly dry feet may benefit from a coating of hoof or vegetable oil following a soak in water as this will trap moisture in but this should always be done in moderation. All the farriers I have spoken to agree a good diet is much more beneficial to the horse's feet than endless applications of hoof oil.

Feed supplements containing biotin and calcium can be given to the horse to help supple up brittle feet, as can a tablespoon of cod-liver oil, olive oil or vegetable oil added to each feed. It is preferable for the condition of the feet to be improved internally rather than externally by improving the diet and maintaining the horse's general condition.

Various treatments are available to harden the hoof, fill cracks and prevent further splitting. They are not intended to compensate for poor shoeing, or to be used on a regular basis. Hoof hardeners are very useful for hardening the surface of the foot so the horseshoe nails can get a better grip, and are painted on like hoof oil. They cannot, however, change the make-up of the foot itself. Most horses get superficial cracks in the hoof wall at some stage or another, and if these start to spread, an adhesive-like substance can be painted around the split to seal it. These work in the same way as gluing a crack in a piece of wood. Larger cracks can be filled with borium or fibreglass compounds and are useful for keeping an even weight-bearing surface should a small piece of the foot come away. Any problems regarding damage to the foot must be dealt with by the farrier, who will suggest a suitable treatment.

# VACCINATIONS

All horses should be vaccinated regularly against Equine Influenza (annually) and Tetanus (at least every two years). Vaccinations work by inducing the production of antibodies within the immunity system by injecting a very small amount of the virus in to the body. As the antibodies fight the viral cells, so the immune system is built up. However, these antibodies die off after a certain length of time so boosters are needed to repeat the process. Both of these injections can be given jointly for practical purposes, though they are also available individually.

All jockey club events and major shows require proof of the initial flu vaccination and yearly boosters, all recorded on a vaccination card, which is completed and signed by the vet when the horse is injected. Due to the fact that many horses travel across the country to these events, and sometimes internationally, the spread of flu is made all too easy. The virus can be spread via airborne particles, so once one horse has contracted it, his companions are likely to as well. Horses who have been vaccinated may still display certain flu symptoms but are unlikely to contract the full-blown virus. Un-vaccinated youngsters are especially at risk as their immune systems are still not fully developed.

Tetanus occurs when germs enter the horse's body through a wound – the tetanus spores may have lain in the ground for years. The disease is very serious as toxic materials within the germs attack the nervous system. Providing the horse has been vaccinated and wounds are cleaned and treated immediately, Tetanus is unlikely. However, it can be fatal, so vaccines and their subsequent yearly or two-yearly boosters are essential.

*All horses should be vaccinated regularly; most major shows and events will require proof that this has been done.*

# DENTAL TREATMENT

Horses' teeth need to be checked regularly, by a vet or equine dentist, for sharp edges and uneven wear. It is difficult for even the most experienced person to check their own horse's teeth, as the molars are too far back to reach without using special gags that keep the mouth open.

If the horse's teeth are too sharp, he cannot chew food properly and it may hinder digestion, causing colic or other digestive problems. A common sign of this is *quidding*, where lumps of food are dropped from the mouth when eating. Problems may also occur when riding, as having a bit in the mouth can cause discomfort if the teeth are sharp. They should be checked

── ECONOMIZE ──

• If using oil to trap moisture in the horse's feet, use vegetable or olive oil. It is cheaper than manufactured brands.
• When feeding liquid supplements and oils to improve the condition of the feet, transfer them to a pump dispenser. This way an equal amount will be distributed daily and wastage will be minimal.
• When booking the vet for vaccinations, see who else requires the vet around at the same time so that call out fees will be reduced.

## FIRE EQUIPMENT

In every yard there should be at least one fire extinguisher, although several extinguishers in accessible places for different types of fires is preferable. All the equipment, including fire blankets, should be checked and serviced annually by the Fire Service.

## GENERAL EQUIPMENT

and rasped if necessary every six months to a year. A good time to do this is when vaccinations are being administered. It is a good idea to keep a diary of all treatments given, for easy reference. When booking appointments, it will be easy to see how much time has elapsed, and there is less chance of forgetting how long ago treatments were given.

The first aid boxes for both equines and humans should be checked every few months and replaced when necessary. General safety checks on facilities such as fencing should be made on a routine basis, and equipment such as tack and rugs should be mended as soon as they are damaged.

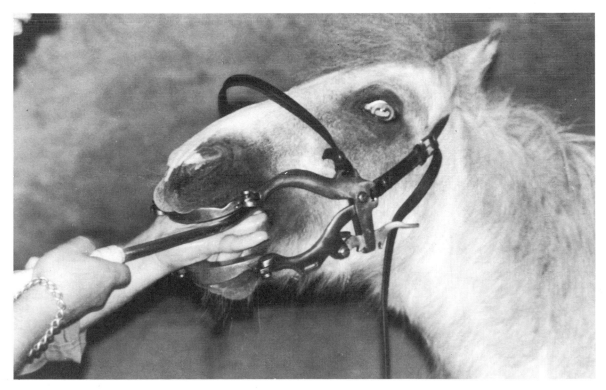

*A vet or equine dentist should check the horse's teeth every six months to a year. The horse should wear a gag for this procedure.*

49

# 4  Feeding

The feeding of horses is a huge and complex subject, owing mainly to the fact that each horse has individual requirements according to their size, age, temperament, health, and the amount of work being done. As such, there are no hard and fast rules that apply to all horses. The art of good, balanced feeding comes with observation and experience.

Horses' diets changed dramatically when they were domesticated by man. Instead of grazing at their leisure for twenty-four hours a day, they were confined to a stable and fed to suit our lifestyle. Developments in feed manufacturing and research followed, including compound feed mixes containing balanced rations, vitamins and minerals. Now with an

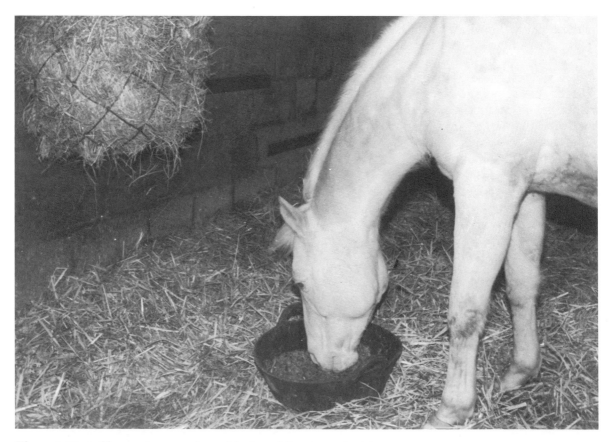

*The nutrition of horses is a complex subject, and it is important to ensure that a correctly balanced diet is provided.*

enormous selection of horse feeds available, choosing what is best for the horse can seem a daunting task, so the first stage is to look at why the horse needs a balanced diet.

## DIETARY REQUIREMENTS

When living in their natural environment, horses can survive perfectly well on a diet of grass and herbs. By stabling them we are asking more of their bodily functions than is required in their natural state, such as burning off more energy and stressing the internal organs. Therefore the feed we give our horses is essential for maintaining a good body temperature and general good condition, providing resources for bodily functions and tissue repair, and supplying energy for the extra work asked of them. The more we ask of our horses through work and fitness, the more 'fuel' their body requires in order to thrive and develop. In a situation where a horse is being underfed, the fuel will be used for the most essential bodily requirement (maintaining body temperature), and condition and energy levels will quickly deteriorate. Overfeeding can result in too much condition, that is fat, and excess energy.

For ease of understanding, feed groups can be divided into three main categories:
1. Concentrated food (cereals, grains, nuts and mixes).
- Proteins to build muscle, repair the body tissues and provide energy. High-protein foods maintain a healthy body for hard work. Horses in light to medium work require between 7 and 9 per cent daily, and performance horses between 10 and 14 per cent.
- Carbohydrates (starches, fibre and sugar) to provide warmth and energy.
- Fats and oils to provide energy stores and insulate the body.
2. Bulk/roughage food high in fibre to stimulate digestion and break up concentrated feeds. Bulk foods include grass, hay, chaff and grass pellets.

3. Auxiliary/additional foods given for a certain purpose, such as to add weight, aid digestion or tempt poor feeders. Auxiliary foods include roots, bran, linseed, fruit and vegetables, and feed additives.

## QUANTITY

It has to be said, the business of working out feed amounts is complicated. As a starting point for assessing the weight of food the horse requires, the daily intake is approximately 25 per cent of the total bodyweight. Finding the bodyweight is the difficult part, as access to weighbridges can prove impractical. Weightapes that estimate the weight according to the size of the barrel (widest part of the belly) are available. A less accurate method of assessing the horse's weight is to use a tape measure and conversion chart. Once the weight is known in kilograms it can be divided by 100, and multiplied by 2.5 to get the daily food intake in kilograms (1kg = 2.2lbs):

$$\frac{Bodyweight}{100} \times 2.5 = \text{capacity in kg}$$

Another, though even less accurate method, is to multiply the horse's height in hands by two, to get an approximation of the daily food intake in pounds. Then divide this by 2.2 to get the food intake in kilograms.

Having estimated the horse's daily food intake, the amount of concentrated and bulk food given can then be worked out. A horse in medium work should get approximately half of each; a horse in very light work approximately one-third concentrates and two-thirds bulk, and a horse in very hard work two-thirds concentrates and one-third bulk.

The whole issue of working out feeding rations is highly confusing, especially as there is a fine line between over- and underfeeding. This is without other aspects being taken into account. For instance, the fact that fit, healthy animals have lower temperatures than their unconditioned counterparts, and so need less fuel to maintain temperature but more to provide energy. Add to this breed characteristics such as high spirits, where fewer energy-giving feeds are needed, and different metabolisms (ability to burn energy) of all horses, and a minefield of considerations is created.

A step-by-step method of working out feeding rationale according to protein value is shown in the section on feeding the performance horse. Though relevant for the horse in hard work, this rationale for concentrate feeds may not be necessary for the horse in light to medium work. In this particular case, I feel prebalanced compound mixes are a lot more practical, and, as they are graded according to nutritional value, there is a mix to suit most horses. Owners simply have to calculate the amount required according to bodyweight (the manufacturer's advice will be on the bag), and then work out how much additional bulk food is needed.

## FEEDING GUIDELINES

There are several guidelines that should be followed to give the horse a healthy and pleasant feeding routine. Obviously a good, balanced diet is desirable, using quality foodstuffs and clean feeding equipment. It is also important to establish a routine, by feeding at regular intervals with no sudden changes in the diet. This is mainly to keep the digestive system running smoothly, as gut bacteria need time to adjust to change, but also because horses find security in routines. They also thrive best when fed little and often. That is to say three smaller feeds are better than two large ones, due to the unnaturally small size of the horse's stomach and nature of the digestive system. It is also necessary for the horse to recover from exercise before being fed, and digest food properly before working. This is because the bodily fluids cannot aid digestion and assist the lungs at the same time, during or after exercise. A rough guide

is to leave at least an hour after feeding before exercise, and thirty minutes after exercise before feeding.

An important guideline to follow is to give a constant supply of fresh, clean water, both in the field and stable. The average horse drinks between 6 and 12 gallons a day. Around 6 of these gallons will be utilized within the body as saliva to aid food consumption and digestion. The water buckets should be filled regularly and changed daily in the stable, as fumes from the bedding will be absorbed. Before and after hard work the horse should not be allowed to drink large amounts, though with a constant supply available he will have a sufficient amount in his body to avoid getting too thirsty or dehydrated.

Water is an essential part of the horse's diet and, in terms of survival, is more important than food. In the wild, horses could survive without food for about a month, but with no water they could die within two weeks.

## CONCENTRATES AND STRAIGHTS

### Oats

Oats are cereal grains with very high energy-giving properties, and they are mainly fed to horses in very hard work, such as racehorses or competition horses. Due to the heating properties of oats, they are not recommended for ponies or horses in light work as they cause undesirable excess energy. They can be fed boiled, which will reduce these properties, though this defeats the object and seems largely a waste of time. When treated, bruised, crushed, rolled or crimped so the husk cracks, they are easily digested, but when fed whole the digestive juices do not penetrate the inner kernel, and the oats lie heavily in the digestive system. They should be clean and dust free, plump and sweet-smelling. Old oats that have lost their nutritional qualities will be small and shrivelled in

*Good-quality oats are clean, plump and sweet-smelling.*

*Whole barley is indigestible, so the husks must be broken before feeding.*

appearance and may smell stale. Once opened, bags of treated oats have a shelf life of only a few weeks. It may be more economical to crush them as required if the bag will not get used up within this time.

Oats have a mineral imbalance, in that they are deficient in calcium and high in phosphorus, because there is a chemical present within them that prevents calcium absorption. There can be up to five times more calcium than phosphorus in a balanced diet, calcium being essential for bone development and blood supply. Too much phosphorus, however, can cause an imbalance between the two minerals and cause bone disease. As oats have a calcium–phosphorus ratio of 1:3, a calcium supplement such as limestone flour or a manufactured alternative can be added to obtain the necessary balance.

## Barley

Barley is an excellent fattening cereal, and though a heating food to a certain degree, it is not to be used for horses in hard work. As the grains are small and, when whole, highly

indigestible, the husks must be broken. This can be done by rolling, flaking or micronizing. Micronizing, or cooking, is preferable as the protein is not lost and the cooked grains are easily digested. Alternatively, barley can be fed boiled, which is even more digestible and the best way for adding weight to horses in

*Barley is excellent for adding weight on to 'poor doers'.*

poor condition. Adequate water should be used when boiling to allow the grains to swell properly, and it should be allowed to cool before feeding. The juices left over from the boiling will be full of nutrition, so they can also be added providing the feed is not too wet.

## Maize

Maize is a very high-energy cereal and also quite fattening. It is only suitable for horses in hard enough work that fat will be burnt off without putting on weight, such as racing or competing. Maize also has low mineral levels, and so is not ideally fed as the main grain ration. Although it can be fed whole, it is usually given in flaked or micronized form.

## Peas and Beans

These are protein-rich pulses, very high in heating and fattening properties. For the same reasons as with maize they are only suitable for horses in hard work and should be fed split or crushed, and not as a main grain ration.

## Compound Cubes and Nuts

Compound cubes and nuts contain cereals and grasses in ground, pelleted form. They are available in varying levels of nutrition from pony nuts to high-performance cubes. The different types contain precise levels of protein, fibre and oil, and as such provide a nicely balanced diet in a convenient and practical form.

However, they are quite unappetizing and dry for the horse, so many owners add extra types of feed to bulk the meal out, or raise the protein levels if low-energy nuts are used. This is fine as long as the nutritional values of the nuts are taken in to account (they will be listed on the bag). By adding different feeds willy-nilly the whole point of giving compound complete foodstuffs will be lost.

The main disadvantage with compound feeds is that the balance has already been made with regard to nutrients and requirements, and cannot be altered except in the amount fed. However, they are very practical to store and do not need mixing, thus saving time for the busy horse owner. There is also the reassurance that the horse's requirements

*Maize is a high-energy feed, and suitable only for horses in hard work.*

*Compound cubes are available in varying levels of nutrition, and convenient to use.*

have already been met by the feed manufac-turers, and any mineral imbalances have been accounted for. It is usually a good idea to dampen nuts before feeding, as when wet they swell a little. If the horse should bolt his feed when dry, the nuts could swell in his stomach and cause discomfort or even colic.

## Coarse Mixes

There are many compound mixes available, with different ingredients and nutritional val-ues. As with nuts and cubes, the mixes are properly balanced to contain essential vitamins and minerals, and quick and practical to use. Most horses seem to prefer mixes to pelleted feeds as they are much more palatable and interesting, and often coated with molasses or some other sweet-tasting binding agent. This also makes them easily digested as they are not too dry, and therefore do not need dampening.

Mixes seem more versatile than nuts and, owing to their growing popularity, there are more variations on the market. Though the balance of the various ingredients in each mix cannot be altered, there is a compound mix to

suit every horse. Owners should look on the feed bag for the breakdown of ingredients. When feeding many horses, the mixes will prove more expensive than buying concen-trate cereals, but for the one-horse owner they are extremely useful. Compound mixes are not intended to have other feeds added, though as with nuts there is no harm adding certain roughage feeds to bulk the meal out if the horse bolts his feed or is in light work.

## BULK OR ROUGHAGE FEEDS

Roughage is essential to the horse's diet, the most natural form being grass.

In the spring and summer, grass is highly nutritious; in fact spring grass is too rich for certain horses, and sometimes needs to be restricted as in excess it can cause serious ill-ness. However, there is rarely enough good grass available to provide the stabled horse with the bulk rations required in the winter, so the grass must be supplemented with addi-tional forage feed:

*Coarse mixes are palatable for the horse, and practical for the owner.*

*Many companies produce their own range of compound feeds and supplements.*

## Hydroponic Grass

Hydroponically produced grass has been marketed as a complementary form of forage. It is grown without soil in large powered units, and is highly succulent and moisture-rich. It is grown from barley seeds, which are similar in nutritional content to spring grass. Unfortunately, the units are practical for use only on a large scale, as they are expensive to buy and run, and as a result, they are not widely used or available. So, while hydroponically grown grass is an innovative idea, traditional roughage feeds are generally still given to provide the necessary bulk.

## Hay

All stabled horses should be fed some form of hay. For some it may only be a quarter of their daily feed intake, but for most horses it is at least one half. The digestive system requires fibrous roughage to function properly, and no other form of roughage can be fed in the large quantities required. Hay is also relatively rich in protein, and contains essential vitamins and minerals.

There are two kinds of traditional hay in common use:
• Seed hay is seeded on arable land and, though quite hard with long stalks, is nutritious.
• Meadow hay, traditionally taken from permanent pasture, is much softer and easier to digest.

All hay should be clean and dust-free in appearance, sweet-smelling with no signs of mould. When buying in large quantities, an analysis can be done to establish the quality, though it is quite impractical for a small amount of bales.

The best hay is usually cut in June, before the grass flowers have scattered their seeds and lost some of their nutrition. The whole business of cutting and baling hay can be dictated by the weather, and an extremely hot or wet summer can influence the quality. Hay that has got wet after being cut will lose some nourishment, and if it is baled while still damp may develop mould and dust spores. Hay that has been 'mowburnt', through early stacking and subsequent heating, will have a brownish tint and will be largely unappetizing to the horse. New hay is bought when it is three to six months old, and between one year and eighteen months old will lose most of its nutritional value and be past its best. Unfortunately there may not be a lot of choice when it comes to purchasing hay, as good hay is often in shortage. In these cases owners must choose the best quality available, even though prices per bale can be as expensive as a bale of shavings.

Dusty hay can be treated to prevent coughs and respiratory problems, though should be discarded if it is very poor. A good method of testing is to shake the hay up in to a pile and if it affects the human respiratory system and results in coughing, then it will affect the horse too. Steaming is the best method, where boiling water is poured over the hay, and then the hay is sealed into a container, making the spores swell to a size where they cannot reach the lungs. Thorough soaking of the hay for a few hours will have the same effect, but dampening has little or no effect at all.

## Haylage

Haylage is vacuum-packed hay, sealed in airtight polythene bags,. It is highly nutritious and totally dust-free. The hay will have been thoroughly dried, then allowed to ferment a little whilst in the bag; though a few bags have been known to be damp and over-fermented, they are largely of good consistent quality. There is a fodder called silage that is treated in a similar way to haylage, though when sealed is not quite dry. The result is a highly fermented hay that is very rich, and not suitable for most horses.

The main disadvantage to haylage is the cost, as it is at least twice the price of a normal bale of hay. However, because of its high nutrition value, you feed less than traditional hay and horses suffering from coughs and respiratory problems will benefit from it. Owners can put it in nets with small mesh holes so the horse will eat less, and to help prevent boredom. Great care must be taken when handling haylage bales because if punctured, the vacuum will be filled with air, and bacteria will grow. Bales should be used within a week of opening.

## Lucerne (Alfalfa)

Lucerne (also known as alfalfa) is a highly nutritious grass, though unfortunately not widely available as baled hay in Great Britain or Europe. Chopped lucerne is more commonly bought in dust-free bagged form, or as compressed grass pellets. Lucerne possesses highly digestible protein and also has a good mineral balance with a high calcium level. This makes it a useful fodder to complement cereals.

## Chaff

Chaff, the name used for most types of chopped hay or straw, adds necessary bulk to feeds, preventing the horse bolting his feed down and also aiding digestion. The majority of manufacturers produce a mixture with around 80 per cent hay and 20 per cent oat straw, though with the use of a chaff-cutter it can be cheaply prepared at home. Molasses is sometimes added to bind the chaff together, and this mixture is known as chop. This is much more palatable for the horse as it is sweet tasting and not too dry, though it has a high sugar content.

## Hay Substitutes

Grass pellets and chopped hay can be used as hay substitutes, though these seem best suited as a short-term measure if there is a hay shortage. One disadvantage is that horses find them boring to eat compared with hay, which when pulled from a haynet can keep horses occupied for hours. Many substitutes will have high protein levels (such as lucerne)

*This roughage feed contains chopped lucerne (alfalfa) grass.*

and will need to be fed in smaller quantities than hay, or the concentrate to bulk feeding ratio will be too high. In the end they may be more expensive, as hay bales, when widely available, are comparatively cheap and long lasting.

*Chopped hay is useful for adding bulk and aiding digestion.*

# AUXILIARY FEEDS

## Sugar Beet Pulp

Sugar beet is a root crop, dried, processed and then soaked before feeding. In cube form it should be soaked in four times its volume of water for twenty-four hours; in shredded form it should be soaked in twice its volume of water for twelve hours. If the sugar beet is not soaked for this length of time before feeding, it will swell dangerously in the horse's stomach and could cause severe colic.

The sugar beet pulp is high in calcium, and is a useful balance for feeds high in phosphorus. It is very bulky and fibrous, thus being excellent for putting weight on horses, as well as being highly palatable. Owing to the high sugar content it is a good energy provider, but when used with molasses feeds can be too sweet, possibly resulting in excess energy or tooth decay. Though useful for horses in low-performance work, it is unsuitable for those in hard or fast work.

## Bran

Bran is a by-product of the milling process, traditionally used to bulk out feeds or as a warm mash for convalescing horses. When added dry to the feed, it is said to have a binding effect on the digestive system; however, it has a poor calcium to phosphorus ratio, because it is excessively high in phosphorus. Though supplements can be added to raise the calcium levels, it seems unnecessary as there are plenty more feeds available that add bulk to the meal without upsetting the mineral balance and tasting so bland.

Though many people still swear by using bran, in my opinion it is of little benefit when used on a daily basis. If the horse's droppings are loose, then a handful or two of bran may help to bind him up, though it seems doubtful that by the time the bran has made its way through the system it will still be dry. There is no doubt that when used in a mash with epsom salts, it is a useful laxative. However, similar mashes can be made just as easily

*Sugar-beet pulp nuts should be soaked in four times their volume of water for twenty-four hours prior to feeding.*

*Bran is traditionally given as part of the bulk ration or as a warm mash.*

with dried grass, a little sugar beet pulp and some epsom salts. Boiling water should be poured over the food until there is a damp consistency, then covered with a cloth or tea towel and allowed to cool to blood temperature. A dried grass and sugar beet mash can be given as a form of warming comfort food for a horse that has lost his appetite and will be a lot more tempting than bran. If used as a laxative, the wet nature of the mash combined with the epsom salts will have just as good an effect, and will also taste better!

## Linseed

Linseed is the seed of the flax plant, and is highly nutritious and rich in oils. It is therefore useful for maintaining condition and adding a gloss to the coat, though impractical to feed as it requires cooking beforehand. When soaked before being boiled and simmered, it forms a jelly which can be added to the daily ration, though feeding over 1lb (550g) in cooked weight is not recommended due to the high protein levels. By adding more water to the seeds when boiling, a tea-like substance will be created which can also be fed to the horse.

The linseed must be thoroughly cooked before feeding, as the un-boiled seeds are poisonous. Though useful at large competition yards where a glossy coat is essential, boiled linseed is time consuming for the one-horse owner. Linseed oil is much simpler to feed and has the same nutritional values. Linseed is present in many high energy compound mixes in the form of cooked and dried cake.

## Soya Bean Meal

Soya bean meal is a very rich feed, suitable for horses in hard work that require the extra protein but will work off the energy. It also adds condition to youngstock, promoting the development of muscle and tissue growth. It is useful when given with corn rations as it contains acids that balance the mineral levels.

## Molasses

Molasses is a by-product of sugar, treacly in consistency and very palatable. It is available in meal or liquid form and is useful for encouraging fussy eaters. Many compound mixes and chopped hay are already coated with molasses to bind the food together and make it more appetizing, so it may be an unnecessary supplement to some foods.

## Succulents

Roots, fruit and vegetables are all excellent succulent foods and can be added to feeds for variety, and as a tasty treat that provides vitamins and minerals. Carrots, apples, swedes, turnips and parsnips are favoured by most horses, and should be chopped lengthways to prevent choking.

## Supplements

There are many vitamin and mineral supplements available on the market, and their purpose is to do just that, supplement. Over-

*Linseed must be cooked before feeding, and is an excellent conditioner.*

*Succulents add variety to the diet, and should be chopped lengthways.*

*Limestone flour is a useful supplement for balancing mineral levels in the diet.*

feeding of supplements can result in a total imbalance of the vitamins and minerals present in the first place. Horses need them to utilize food properly and maintain healthy bones and organs. Many vitamins complement and work with minerals, so their balance is important. Certain supplements are used to improve certain aspects of the horse's make up. For instance, biotin for healthy feet and cod liver oil to promote tissue and bone growth. Before purchasing any supplement it is worth consulting an equine nutritionist

first. Owners may be doing more harm than good, or just wasting their money.

**Salt** This plays an important role in the horse's development and is essential for the breakdown of protein in the diet. A little can be added daily in the feed, though most compound feeds contain the required amount. Salt-licks can also be provided in the stable and field, and most horses will take advantage of them if salt is lacking in their diet.

**Electrolytes** These are a form of salt naturally present in the horse's body that balances the fluids and minerals. Manufactured versions are given to horses in order to rebalance their own electrolytes following dehydration and sweating. They are commonly added to the water following racing or endurance riding, though prevention of dehydration and profuse sweating is important. Electrolytes are used to complement good management, not to replace it.

**Milk pellets** These are useful additives for youngstock, or horses that heat up on high-protein feeds. They are highly nutritious and protein-rich, and though relatively expensive are excellent for building up horses in poor condition that could not cope with a high level of concentrates.

*Herbal Supplements*

There are many different herbal supplements available which are designed to provide the specific benefits of herbs in palatable formulations such as liquid and powder. Some of the most common natural additives include garlic, to aid respiration and cleanse the blood, and comfrey to promote tissue repair and ease rheumatism. In my own experience I have found most of the natural additives extremely useful, especially calming mixes containing camomile or hops. Providing the plants were not sprayed with pesticide prior to cutting, they are also safer to feed than chemically produced alternatives, as there is little chance of overdosing.

*Other Supplements*

Some horses will even benefit from supplements from a human's feed store, such as eggs for an all-round conditioner, beer for a pick-me-up tonic and olive oil for a shiny coat. They are usually given as a special tonic before an event, or a few days before a show, and may counteract or slow the effects of other supplements if given on a long-term basis.

# FOOD STORAGE

Many feeds go stale after a week or two of being opened and if left in contact with the air will then lose some of the nutritional content. To avoid this, store feed in airtight containers, which will also keep it clean, dry and away from vermin. Any airtight container will be suitable providing it is of a suitable depth and size. For the one- or two-horse owner, plastic dustbins are ideal containers as they hold enough for a few weeks' supply of food and are easily lifted. Old open-top freezers are also useful as they have good seals and are definitely vermin-proof. It may be difficult to clean out large containers, but this must be

| Typical Nutritional Values Of Common Foodstuffs | | | | |
|---|---|---|---|---|
| Food | Protein(%) | Oil(%) | Fibre(%) | Sugar(%) |
| Oats | 11 | 5 | 12 | – |
| Barley | 11 | 2 | 5 | – |
| Maize | 10 | 4 | 2 | – |
| Peas & beans | 25 | 1.5 | 9 | – |
| *Horse & pony cubes | 11 | 3 | 14 | ** |
| *Horse & pony mix | 10.5 | 2.75 | 12.5 | ** |
| Hydroponic grass | 16 | 4 | 12 | – |
| Average hay | 8 | 1.6 | 35 | – |
| Haylage | 16 | 2.5 | 30 | – |
| Lucerne | 11.5 | 2.5 | 25.0 | – |
| Chaff | 8 | 1.6 | 35 | ** |
| Sugar beet pulp | 10 | 0.5 | 15 | 22 |
| Bran | 25 | 1.5 | 9 | – |
| Linseed | 26 | 39 | 6 | – |
| Soya bean meal | 50 | 1 | 6 | – |
| Molasses | 14 | 1.75 | – | 37.8 |
| Carrots | 15 | – | 8 | – |
| Milk pellets | 23 | 15.5 | – | – |

Nutritional values will vary according to manufacturer and grading.
* These figures correspond to low-energy compound feeds for horses in light work.
** Sugar content will be considerable if molasses is included in compound.

done otherwise old feed will stay beneath new feed and not get used up. It is a good idea to place containers on palettes or blocks, so excess feed is easily swept up, discouraging vermin and creating a clean environment.

The feed store should be secured so there is no chance of horses entering and gorging on

61

food. This is especially dangerous if a horse gets to the sugar beet, which if eaten dry will swell in the stomach. Easy access for delivery is important, with a door wide enough to carry large bales through.

Baled food such as hay should be kept in a dry environment, as once it gets wet it will develop fungal spores. A spare stable is an ideal place, though anywhere with decent shelter will suffice. Hay should be stored on palates too if possible, as this will discourage vermin from nesting in the bales and will prevent any damp from the floor affecting the bales. It is possible to store hay outside on palettes if covered with tarpaulin, though in bad rain some of the bales are bound to get wet. Once they are damp, they can ferment under the tarpaulin, and in hot weather they may develop further spores.

## FEEDING THE PERFORMANCE HORSE

Horses in hard work burn up a lot of energy, and their internal organs and muscles are put under extra strain. This means the fuel we give them must be specially designed to cope with the stress of hard work, and contain sufficient feeding levels. Cereal foods with high protein levels will produce starch, which is required by the horse's body to convert into physical energy. The vitamins and minerals present within the diet will also need to cope with the strain of work, as the blood and muscles work harder to maintain fitness.

Although the daily food intake will be roughly the same as for the horse in light to medium work, the contents of the feed will differ. As we have already seen, horses in medium work will probably require an equal amount of concentrate and roughage feeds, whereas performance horses will require approximately two-thirds concentrate and one-third roughage. Having decided how much concentrated feed the horse requires, the amount of protein in the diet can be considered. Horses in

hard work (that is, working at fast paces or for long amounts of time every day) will require between 10 and 14 per cent protein though the individual requirements will have to be taken into account.

There are two ways to feed the performance horse – using high energy compound feeds specifically balanced to provide the correct amount of protein, or straight foods bought separately. A well-balanced feed will allow the horse in hard work to perform at his very best, the opposite will see him losing energy or condition, so a suitable and carefully worked out feeding programme is essential. The best way to do this is to sit down with pen and paper and write everything down including weight, height, age, temperament and, of course, work being done. Then the daily intake should be worked out,

$$\frac{Bodyweight}{100} \times 2.5 =$$

and an assessment made of how much protein is required for the horse to perform well, (between 10 and 14 per cent). Then a list should be made of high protein feeds. Does the horse bolt some, dislike others or get especially heated on certain types? What is practical to use and readily available from local feed stockists? By narrowing down the types of feed, owners will be left with a shortlist. The next stage, having chosen the types of food most suited to the horse, is to allocate foodstuffs by weight.

For example, here is an imaginary horse: a fit, 16hh, ten-year-old hunter of even temperament weighs 10cwt (500kg), and requires approximately 27.5 lb (12.5kg) of food per day. As he is in hard work, I choose to give him 17½lb (8kg) concentrates, and 10lb (4.5kg) roughage. In my opinion he requires 10 per cent protein per day. His personal shortlist of suitable foods are:
• Hay (containing 8 per cent protein).
• Chaff (containing 8 per cent protein).
• Nuts (containing 9 per cent protein).
• Oats (containing 11 per cent protein).

- Maize (containing 10 per cent protein).
- Linseed (containing 26 per cent protein).

Following these calculations, it is a matter of dividing the foodstuff by weight into practical amounts (according to their properties and values) and noting their protein level:

# FEEDING THE HORSE AT GRASS

The main difference between feeding stabled horses and those permanently living out lies in their fuel requirements, particularly during

| Food | Weight (kg) | | Protein content (%) | | Protein in ration (g) |
|---|---|---|---|---|---|
| Hay | 4 | × | 8 | = | 32 |
| Chaff | 0.5 | × | 8 | = | 4 |
| Nuts | 3 | × | 9 | = | 27 |
| Oats | 3 | × | 11 | = | 33 |
| Maize | 1.5 | × | 10 | = | 15 |
| Linseed | 0.5 | × | 26 | = | 13 |
| | 12.5 | | | | 124 |

By multiplying 12.5 (daily intake) and 10 (required daily protein percentage) we get an estimate of the total amount of protein required daily in grams:

12.5 × 10 = 125g

As we can see, the protein in the ration (124g) falls within the estimate of the amount of protein required daily (125g). It must not be more than the second figure, as it will then exceed the required amount.

The final calculation is to weigh the feed being given so the amounts given are accurate, and divide the daily intake by the amount of feeds being given, as it is worked out per day, not per feed.

The above is just an example based on an imaginary horse. Other horses of a similar size may burn off energy more quickly and may have different protein requirements. There will always be a small amount of trial and error involved; after all the art of feeding is learned through experience. The horse must be carefully observed when on a new feeding regime, to see if he is losing or gaining condition and coping with the work asked of him. All food should be gradually introduced so the gut becomes accustomed to it, and fed in small quantities for ease of digestion.

Without a doubt it is advisable to consult an equine nutritionist when planning a feeding rationale, even if it is in order to confirm the suitability of a feeding chart already worked out at home. Feed stockists and manufacturers will have details of this service.

the winter. While we take care of the stabled horse's temperature with rugs and thick bedding, those living out have different requirements. Although some may need to be rugged in the cold weather, their rugs prohibit movement and comfort, and therefore they should not be be thick and heavy like some stable rugs. Horses living out are able to exercise in the field to keep warm and should have adequate shelter, but the majority of their warmth comes from the inside and not from artificial heating. The point being, the prime utility of their food is to maintain temperature.

No hard working horse in the winter can live out, be clipped, keep warm, maintain fitness and perform at his best. Therefore, the horse at grass will be resting or in light to medium work, and his feeding programme will consist of between half and two-thirds of roughage. If he is worked, he will need a small amount of energy-giving feed to maintain condition and health, and this can be worked out using the same feeding rationale as for the stabled horse, though obviously more of the food will be used to keep warm. If feeding straight foods, barley and sugar beet pulp are both good for maintaining condition whilst providing protein. High-protein foods should be avoided, and plenty of bulk such as chaff given within the ration. However, in my opinion, compound foods will prove the most practical in this instance, and with a generous supply of hay will provide a suitable diet.

If the horse is resting, then a low protein maintenance diet is all that is required. An

*Performance horses need a specially designed diet as they burn off extra energy.*

*ad-lib* supply of hay can be given to supplement the grass and provide the bulk, which in winter will have little nutritional value. Grass nuts, chaff and grass substitutes can all be given, up the limit of 25 per cent of the bodyweight.

In the summer, if the horse is resting, a diet of good grass will be enough to maintain health and condition, providing it is in plentiful supply. Horses living out are able to maintain fitness in the summer as they do not need to utilize the food for warmth. Their feeding programme can be worked out in the same way as if they were stabled. However, it is important their grass is restricted, as if they consume more than their designated amount of roughage, they will put on weight and therefore not perform as well as they might. Spring grass is too rich in large amounts for many horses anyway, and if consumed in excess along with concentrate foods is downright dangerous. The bloodstream will be filled with protein and may cause serious ailments. Fencing off parts of the paddock with electric fencing could be the answer, or turning the horse out on a bare starvation paddock with minimal grass.

---

**ECONOMIZE**

- Water buckets can be cheaply bought from builders merchants or garden centres.
- If flexible rubber bowls split, they can be repaired by making holes either side of the crack, and lacing upwards with bailer twine in the same way as shoe laces.
- Even though haynets are reasonably cheap nowadays, it may still be worth making your own as, apart from anything else, you will be able to 'custom-make' it to your precise requirements.

  Start with twenty-five strings. Plait three together (preferably a different colour from the rest) for the tying-up string, knot the remaining twenty-two together and hang the knot up with the strings hanging below. Working in pairs going around the circumference of the knot, tie two strings together using a reef knot. When all the strings are knotted, move down and repeat the process. Diamond shapes will be created, and the distance between the knots will determine the size of the diamonds. (Nets with smaller holes will slow down eating.) When all the strings are knotted to the end, the plaited string can be threaded through. Knots can be carefully sealed with a small flame to prevent fraying.
- Cheap feed scoops can be made by cutting a large plastic water bottle to the desired shape and filing the rough edges. The bottle handle is used as the scoop handle.

# 5 Turnout

## GROOMING

Daily attention to the stabled horse's coat is essential because grooming promotes health by removing dead skin cells, improves blood circulation, and tones muscles. It also ensures cleanliness and improves the appearance of the horse. Appearance is often considered the most important by some proud owners, though the horse's skin is not there for cosmetic reasons. It forms a protective, sensitive, regenerative layer over the body and regulates temperature. There are two layers of skin: the outer epidermis, and the sensitive under-layer of dermis. The epidermis consists of dead cells, which flakes into dandruff just like human cells. Living cells are then produced by the dermis, which in turn die off and flake in to the hair to complete the cycle. The dermis itself is very sensitive to pressure as it contains nerve endings, so it must be treated gently during grooming. It also contains blood capillaries that regulate temperature, constricting to conserve heat and expanding to cool the horse down. Waste products from the body are also removed via the skin, through tiny pores. After sweating, the pores may get blocked, therefore it is important to wash away any sweat by sponging the horse down.

Grooming is itself a form of massage, so the capillaries and blood flow will be stimulated, thus raising the temperature. The muscles will also be toned to a certain extent. Hand rubbing is also beneficial, easing tired muscles and releasing tension. Grooming and massaging are also excellent ways of bonding with young or nervous horses, so they form an important part of the handling process.

The term 'grooming' is used to cover a range of techniques, from a quick going over to remove any surface mud, known as brushing off, to a total cleaning and toning session. In previous years a thorough grooming was given to each horse daily, usually administered by a groom responsible for only a few horses and with ample time to spare. Before exercise the horse was *quartered*, the stable rugs folded forwards or backwards and the corresponding body area brushed and tidied up. After exercise, when the skin was warm and supple, an hour-long grooming and toning session known as *strapping* was given. In the past, horses spent more time in potentially dusty stables and less time exercising in the field. Horses that are allowed plenty of natural toning exercise and a good roll to loosen excess scurf and dead cells are probably no worse off in the long run than their pampered friends. Though strapping is undoubtedly beneficial for the horse, nowadays few people can spare either the time or resources. Even grooms in large yards today tend to have more horses to look after, and so have to resort to more time-saving methods.

Grooming machines save time and are hygienic to use. Dirt and scurf is vacuumed up into the machine, so it does not float around in the air only to fall back on the horse. The machines also come with various motor sizes, from huge, heavy duty models to small lightweight versions suitable for the one-horse owner, and with various versatile brushes that fit at the end of a flexible tube. Though initially some horses may be alarmed at the noise, most really enjoy the sensation of an electric groomer as it massages and relaxes the muscles. Some older models are heavy and cumbersome to use, and need careful handling in case they bang against the horse and hurt him. Lightweight groomers are much easier to use and control, especially on high speeds. Care must be taken when using revolving cleaning brushes as opposed to flat, toning versions, because long hair, whether it be human or equine, can get caught up around the bristles. For this reason, the mane should be brushed out of the way and the tail bandaged, as once hairs become entangled they are difficult to remove.

## The Grooming Kit

Using the traditional grooming kit is more time-consuming, but helps to develop a more personal relationship with the horse and is useful for brushing off. The grooming kit consists of:

**Dandy brush** A stiff bristled brush, used for removing mud and sweat from the limbs and body of the horse in winter. Using the dandy brush when the horse has a thin summer coat, or on areas that have been clipped may damage the skin.

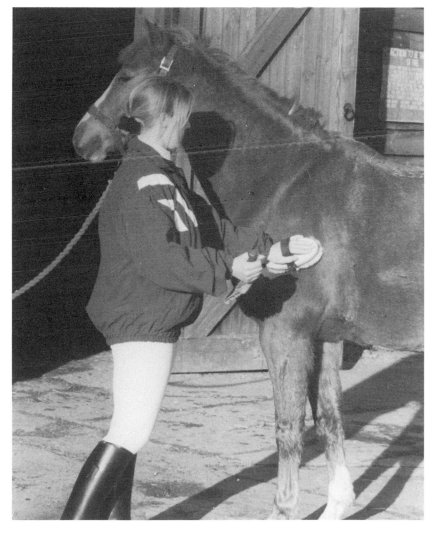

*Daily grooming will not only promote health and appearance, but is an important part of the handling process.*

Some thin-skinned horses may find the bristles too harsh whatever the season, so the dandy brush must be used gently. It should not be administered on the sensitive facial area, or the tail as it will pull out or split hairs.

**Body brush** A soft, short-bristled brush used for removing grease and scurf from all over the body. It is suitable for use on the more sensitive areas including the face, and will not damage tail hairs. It is used in conjunction with the curry-comb.

**Metal curry-comb** A tool with rows of metal teeth used for cleaning the body brush. It is used during grooming following a build-up of dirt on the brush, the contents knocked off the comb onto the floor, or into a skip.

**Plastic curry comb** A brush for use on the limbs or body of the horse in winter. It is very useful for removing caked dirt and mud as it has rows of pointed teeth. It is unsuitable for use on sensitive areas or tail hair for the same reasons as the dandy brush. It can also be used to clean dirt build-up from the body brush.

**Rubber curry comb** A small brush with rows of blunt teeth, used to loosen and remove dirt and unwanted hair. It is especially useful when the horse is losing his thick winter coat, and is also a good muscle toner.

**Water brush** A soft version of the dandy brush, used to dampen down mane and tail hair prior to plaiting; it can also be used with care on the face.

*Using the traditional grooming kit is time consuming, but aids bonding between horse and owner.*

**Mane comb** This is used for combing out the mane when plaiting, or pulling the mane and tail. It should not be used daily to tidy the mane and tail as the hairs can be damaged.

**Hoof-pick** A metal or plastic tool to remove dirt and mud from the feet. Versions with brushes on the end for cleaning the hooves are very useful.

**Hoof oil** An optional extra, this is used for adding a sheen to the hooves or moisture to dry and brittle feet.

**Sponges/moist tissues** Used for cleaning the delicate eye, nostril, and lip areas, and also the horse's dock and sheath. Moist tissues, the kind used for babies, are much more hygienic than sponges and can be discarded straight away; the unperfumed ones are preferable. If using sponges, a separate one must be used around the dock and sheath to prevent the spread of germs. Larger sponges are useful when bathing, or sponging the horse down.

**Stable rubber/cloth** This removes surface dust on the coat after grooming. Any cloth, such as a tea towel will be suitable, though cotton wears thin with heavy use.

**Banger/massage pad** There are several pads available for toning muscle, from leather or sheepskin to rubber or nylon. Bangers are used to stimulate muscle development, whereas massage pads relax and supple the muscles, but both improve circulation. Wisps (thick home-made loops of hay or straw) are also used for a similar purpose and stimulate the skin to produce a shiny coat.

**Sweat-scraper** A tool for removing water from the horse's body following sweating or bathing. There are two versions available, either rubber- or metal-edged.

## Grooming Procedure

The horse should be tied up or, if in the stable, given a haynet to keep him occupied. The rugs should then be removed, or in cold weather laid over the quarters so the horse does not chill. The feet should be picked out and brushed, and surplus dirt removed from the body with the dandy brush, though thin-skinned horses may find this too abrasive. The body brush is then used with firm strokes along the coat, so the dirt is removed from the roots, and then brushed out against the curry-comb approximately every six strokes. The face is also groomed with the body brush, the eyes, nose and dock cleaned, and the mane and tail brushed out and laid flat.

The summer coat can be wiped over with a cloth to remove surface dirt, and hoof oil added if desired. The sheath needs to be cleaned with a sponge periodically. Some horses require this weekly, but most only every few months.

If the horse is losing his winter coat, the rubber curry-comb can be used before the dandy brush to remove excess hair. There is little point using the body brush at this stage as it will just get clogged up with hair. Most of the scurf will fall out too, so it is a case of leaving the coat to its own devices. Endless grooming and polishing will be fruitless, as the next day another layer of hair and skin cells will fall out.

It makes little difference in which order the parts of the body are groomed and comes down to personal preference and efficiency, though if the feet are to be oiled they should be picked out and brushed first so they have time to dry.

When the horse has been groomed, there are various methods of toning and massaging the muscles. Banging is usually done when the horse is strapped, and a thick pad is literally banged against the horse's body so the muscles flinch and then relax. Though banging will improve physique to a certain extent, I question whether it is wise to build a gentle relationship with the horse whilst grooming, and then systematically hit him. Obviously banging is not supposed to hurt and is for the horse's benefit, but in my opinion it only serves to alarm most horses. In order to make a substantial difference to the muscle development, banging must be administered frequently and for long periods of time. It would seem a much less time-consuming and drastic measure to give a suitable muscle-building exercise programme, and daily massage with a rubber curry-comb and soft pad. The rubber brushes used with an electric groomer are excellent for toning muscle, so purchasing a machine may be an investment if muscle tone is necessary but cannot be achieved just through schooling, such as for in-hand young show stock. Using a grooming machine to tone muscle is much more efficient than banging, and I suspect it is also a great deal more pleasant for the horse.

Ideally, thorough grooming should be administered after exercise, as at this time the pores will be open and the skin therefore easy to clean. However the horse must be dry, as sweat could be brushed back in to the skin causing discomfort and irritation. The average grooming time is around fifteen minutes, though of course this will depend on the state of the horse's coat and the time of year. If owners are pushed for time, it is quite acceptable just to pick out the feet and give a quick brushing off to remove the surface mud before riding, providing a thorough grooming is given the next day.

## Maintaining Condition

In order for the horse's skin and coat to remain healthy it must be properly looked after. For instance, field-kept horses do not require daily grooming, though they should have their feet picked out regularly and be brushed off with a dandy brush prior to riding. The grease in their coat will provide a waterproof, insulating layer and removal with a body brush will be detrimental to their welfare. However, stable-kept horses must be groomed regularly as dirt from the field, and sweat from exercising should not be allowed to accumulate. The result will be blocked pores and a dull coat, and skin irritations and saddle sores from tack or clothing and dirt rubbing together. The effect of saddle sores can be long lasting and painful, and their appearance can be seen as a form of neglect.

There are several products available to improve the horse's condition cosmetically, including coat sheens and glosses. They are mainly used for shows, softening the hair and making the coat slippery. This can hinder plaiting and may make saddles slip, but when used on the tail it will be much easier to brush and may appear thicker.

The horse's skin glands produce a natural lubricant when healthy, so the best way to keep the coat in good condition is to groom regularly and provide a good diet. Certain feed supplements and oils will induce more of the natural lubricant from the glands, these being preferable to glosses, as in the same way as hoof treatments it is better for the condition to be improved from the inside than outside.

The grooming equipment must be kept clean, and ideally should be washed weekly. This is mainly for hygiene reasons and to prevent the spread of disease, but also as the brushes will not do their job properly if they are dirty. Warm soapy water will do the trick, though brushes with wooden or leather bases should not be left to soak in the water. A clean plastic curry-comb can be used with water to clean the bristles of the dandy, body and water brushes, which when rinsed should be left to dry, bristles down for good drainage. A scrubbing or nail brush is useful for cleaning curry-combs. All grooming equipment should be rinsed thoroughly in case any residue is left on the bristles and transferred to the horse's skin, and cloths and stable rubbers washed regularly to prevent the spread of germs.

As previously discussed, grooming and massage is useful for stimulating muscles and blood flow. Horses can be treated with machines to improve their circulation and muscle tone, though on veterinary advice during rehabilitation and not as a matter of course. Some simply massage and stimulate a sore area, such as hand held mechanical massagers that vibrate against the skin; others, such as veterinary muscle stimulators, attach via electrodes to the body sending an electrical current to the desired area.

# BATHING THE HORSE

Bathing horses is more common nowadays than in past years, and some competition horses are bathed all year round. Without proper drying facilities, it is unwise to bath horses in the winter, and most do not require it anyway because their coat grease serves as an insulator that should not be removed. Many people bath their horses too frequently, especially in the summer months when there are shows and events to go to. It is not so much the action of bathing – which is beneficial and

enjoyable for most horses – but the drying effects of the cleaning product that cause problems. Most shampoos contain harsh soap, which if not properly washed out can be uncomfortable and itchy for the horse. Equine or baby shampoos seem the best type, and very mild medicated versions are useful for the horse with a scurfy coat. If the horse is being bathed to remove surface dirt, no product is necessary; the water will do the job sufficiently and will not break down the grease.

When bathing, it is important to have a good supply of water. In the summer when the weather is quite warm, cold hose water will be

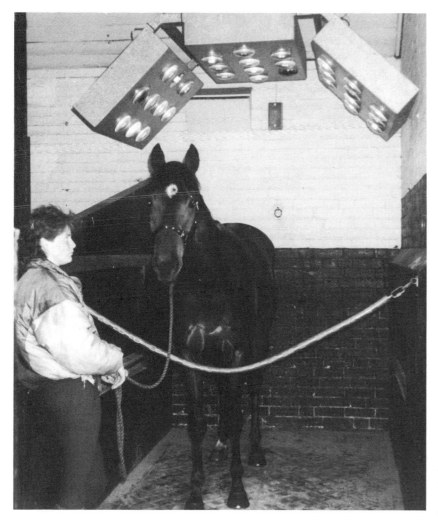

*Horses may be bathed at any time of year providing there are proper drying facilities*

71

adequate, though warm water is preferable. If the water is previously boiled, it must have cooled right down to blood temperature (100.5°F/38°C), with plenty available for rinsing. A water heater is another option, especially if the thermostat can be set so the running water is the desired temperature. This will make bathing in slightly colder weather possible, as if both the bathing water and the air temperature are cold the horse will not be able to warm his body sufficiently and may chill.

It is useful to have a stable or area used specifically for bathing, with good drainage and practical access to water. There is nothing worse than reams of hosepipe across the yard getting in the way, or having to walk long distances with buckets of water, most of which is lost on the way. A stable or concrete area can be easily swept out afterwards, but gravel or soil quickly becomes messy and waterlogged.

The horse should be thoroughly wet before shampooing, with small amounts of shampoo applied to the hands and then massaged into the coat. Applying the shampoo directly to the horse may result in difficult removal and consequent irritation. The coat should be vigorously massaged with the fingers to produce a good lather and to loosen all the dirt and excess grease. The spine will probably be the dirtiest and will need special attention, as will those areas most difficult to reach, such as the chest and belly. If only slightly damp before shampooing, the soap will not lather and subsequently may not be properly rinsed. This is where a hosepipe is useful. The mane and tail can be washed along with the body, though I find it easiest to leave the head until last to wash separately. Shampooing should be done quickly, so the coat does not begin to dry before rinsing, and all the suds should be thoroughly washed away, with several rinses given if necessary. A special brush fitted via an attachment to a hose will be useful, as it will massage the skin and remove excess suds and stubborn dirt. Special attention should again be paid to the chest and belly area, where gravity makes rinsing more difficult.

The head will not require too much shampoo, as the lather will get into the eyes and sting. Baby shampoo is the best type to use and should be rinsed carefully, making sure no water gets into the ears.

A sweat-scraper is used next on the body, in long, firm strokes to remove excess water. Water is removed from the legs, either by running the hands down them, or by looping twine around the leg and gently pulling down. If the legs are not dried properly there is a high risk of skin irritation or disease, especially if the horse has thick feathers around the fetlock joint. A sweat rug under a summer sheet or a large towel can then be put over the horse to dry him off, though in warm weather he will dry quickly if simply walked around. Chest, belly and leg areas can be towel dried, and even hair-dryers can be used if earthed and plugged in to a circuit breaker. They must be used on a low setting, and not too close to sensitive areas as they may be too hot. Wicking rugs and leg wraps are useful in colder weather, as they draw moisture away from the horse to the outer layer of the material. Infra-red drying lamps are also excellent for quick drying, though impractical for the average horse owner. In larger yards with access to heat lamps, horses will dry quickly in the comfort of a stable even in cold weather. Bathing is safe in colder weather providing the water used is at blood temperature, and the horse is properly dried off. He can be lightly lunged or lead around in his drying rugs, and also energetically hand-rubbed to stimulate circulation and heat.

Certain parts of the horse, such as the sheath, mane and tail, may need washing more frequently. The gelding's sheath should be sponged with warm water, taking great care to be gentle in case he should kick out. The most suitable products are manufactured sheath cleaning gels, which break down any build-up in an easy-to-rinse form. If the horse objects it may be wise to have an assistant at hand to hold a foreleg to prevent kicking and to calm the horse down.

The mane and tail can be washed quite regularly and they will both dry quickly, though the neck should not be made too soapy and wet. Grey tails often get exceptionally dirty, and these may be washed with gentle soap flakes in order to remove any stubborn stains. A colour enhancing 'blue bag' rinse was used to great effect on tails for some years, to give the blue-white colour intended for home washing. However, it is notoriously difficult, if not absolutely impossible, to get hold of now. Washing powder detergents claiming to whiten whites should be avoided, as they are too harsh for use on horses, and irritate the skin on the dock.

## PULLING AND TRIMMING

Manes and tails are trimmed and tidied up by various means, for the ease of plaiting and general management, and to improve the appearance of the horse. The extent to which the horse is tidied up depends largely on the breed type and situation. For instance, many Arabs and native breeds with fine hair are left with long manes and tails, at competitions the manes being put in a single plait down the neck. Field-kept horses that are never plaited up will need plenty of hair as protection against flies and cold, and excess removal of hair is unnecessary. Personal preference is involved, too: some people prefer their horses to have the natural look, while others opt for a tidier one.

Pulling is a method of shortening and thinning the mane and tail, where the hair from the underside is pulled out in small sections. It is best done after exercise, as the pores and hair follicles will be warm, and the hair will come out more easily. When pulling the mane, all the hair is thoroughly combed out so it lies flat. Then taking a mane comb, small sections of the hair are back-combed to the root, and literally pulled out. It is important to pull out only a small amount of hair at any one time, otherwise the process will be painful. Some horses that have had bad experiences during mane pulling are touchy or even head shy for the rest of their lives. Working along the length of the neck, the mane is thinned and shortened until it is the desired thickness and

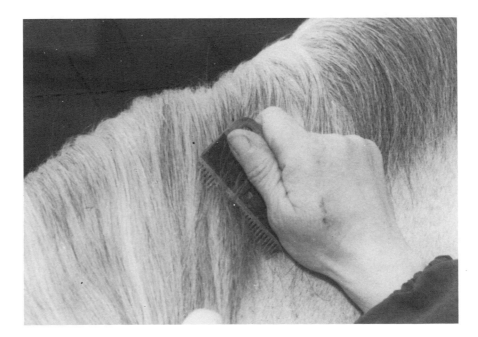

*Before pulling, the mane is brushed or combed flat.*

73

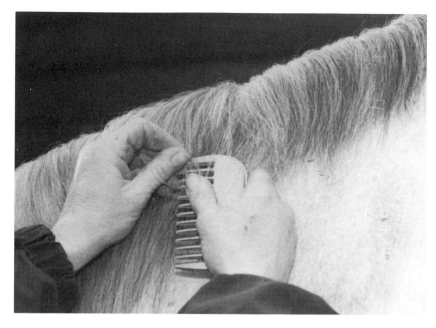

*A small section of hair is backcombed ...*

length. About 4in (10cm) is a practical length for plaiting. The mane will need to be pulled a little every few weeks to stay at this length, and if done frequently, in small amounts, it is easy to manage.

However, I do feel pulling has its disadvantages, including being distressing for some horses and quite time-consuming. Personally,

I prefer to use other methods of tidying the mane. It seems to me that many of the horses who have pulled manes for plaiting are types with fine, thin hair. It is quite practical in these cases where the manes need shortening rather than thinning, to back-comb the hair then trim the underside with scissors. A neat, level hairline is achieved with minimal fuss.

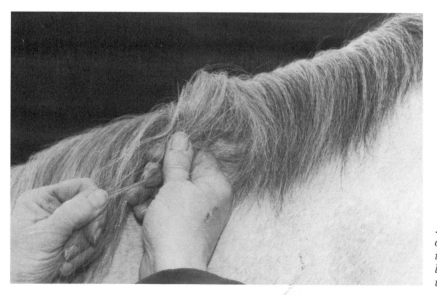

*... and then literally pulled out. Using the fingers instead of a comb may be less painful for those horses who object.*

Alternatively, a thinning or razor comb can be used, a handy device with a row of double teeth concealing a blade. They are quite safe to use and available from most chemists. When back-combed the hair is thinned, when angled forward and combed downwards it is shortened. They are not suited to reducing long manes, but are practical for tidying up short ones and take little time. If a long mane is to be shortened, I see nothing wrong with cutting the excess off with scissors then tidying the mane using whichever method is preferred. Problems only occur when using scissors if the ends of the mane are blunt. Providing the underside is thinned and the mane tidied it will look neat and smart. The forelock is maintained in the same way as the mane, though care must be taken around the horse's eyes if using scissors or a razor comb. It may be useful to stand on something solid, as guesswork from below the head will result in a messy forelock.

Tail pulling is done in much the same way as the mane, a few hairs at a time taken from the top of the tail at the sides to give a neat, tapered effect down the dock. These tails are not plaited, and if properly managed look quite smart. However, some horses do not appreciate the action of tail pulling, as the dock area is sensitive, much more so than the hairline of the neck. There is also the disadvantage that once the hair is pulled it must be regularly maintained, as it will take years for the hairs to grow long enough to stay in a plait and meantime will resemble a scrubbing brush. Once again I prefer not to pull tails, and think a neat plait looks much nicer. The end of the tail will need trimming every few months, and is generally cut straight across giving a level finish. A good length for the tail is approximately 4in (10cm) below the hock joint, though slightly higher is quite acceptable. When trimming, it is easiest to let the tail hang over your shoulder, running the other hand down the hair and stopping at the desired length. It should be trimmed in this raised position so when the horse lifts his tail during exercise it will not be too short. The remaining hair below the hand is then cut off with a sharp pair of scissors. Tail hair that is tapered to a natural point at the ends is known as a switch tail, and is not favoured by many due to its unkempt appearance.

## Trimming Excess Hair

There are several areas of the body that are scissor trimmed to remove excess hair, usually for cosmetic reasons. These are around the ears, muzzle and jaw, bridle path or top notch (where the bridle and headcollar lie on the mane), and around the fetlocks. Trimming the head area is done for appearance in showing classes, yet many people who do not compete still trim the sensitive muzzle and whisker hairs, and even the feeler hairs around the eye. This seems quite unnecessary as the hairs are there for a purpose. Some horses will be disorientated by a sudden lack of feeling sensors, and may be more cautious about eating their food. The same goes for the ears, where some show horses have the visible inside hair trimmed away, even though this may allow dirt and foreign bodies inside the ear. However, straggly outer hairs can be carefully trimmed, and the protruding hairs from inside cut level with the outer edge of the ear.

Hair around the jaw line is usually trimmed to show off the shape of the head, as it can grow quite long and will give the appearance of an untidy beard. In previous years it was singed to give a natural finish, though this seems highly dangerous and impractical when an acceptable outline can be achieved with a pair of scissors.

The feather hair around the fetlock can be trimmed for appearance, or if it is too thick and retains moisture. A comb is used in the opposite direction to the coat, and the excess hair outside the comb cut and shaped around the bone. Care must be taken not to produce what looks like steps of hair that are uneven, or trim too much away so there is not enough protection or drainage when the leg is wet.

## PLAITING

The mane and tail are plaited for competitive events and hunting, purely to give an orderly, smart appearance. Fashions change over the years, and for a while it was customary to have an odd number of plaits down the neck, usually nine or eleven, the forelock plait creating an even number. Considering the fact that some horses have long necks, this was no mean feat, and occasionally resulted in heavy plaits that made the horse's neck look thick. Nowadays most people have as many plaits as is practical, and in a range of styles. Usually the plaits are rolled into small balls, though on longer manes the plaits can be folded into sausage shapes.

Someone with an experienced eye can plait as they go, dividing a small section at a time, plaiting to the end and then rolling up from the top of the neck before securing. To be sure of an even amount of hair in each plait, the mane can first be divided into sections and secured which, though time-consuming, ensures consistency. The plaits are either secured with needle and thread, which look

*Prior to plaiting, the mane should be brushed or combed out, and then divided into sections.*

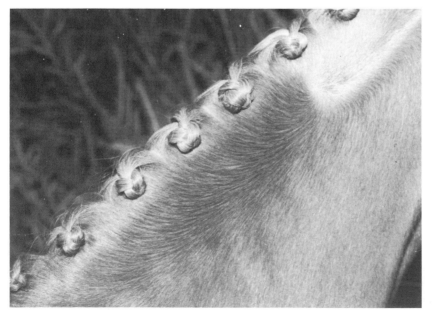

*Fashions in plaiting may change, but a row of neat, orderly plaits always looks smart.*

*Tail plaiting.*

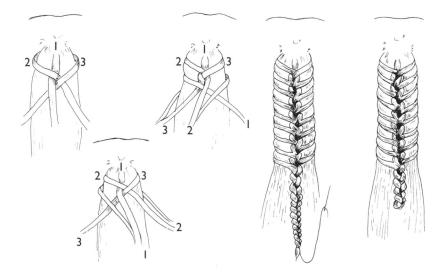

smart and will stay in place, or elastic bands that are efficient but don't always look as professional. Elastic bands seem best suited for one or two classes at an event, and thread for a whole day's work such as hunting.

One attractive method when using single plaits is to do each as an individual **French pleat**. This involves dividing part of the section of mane in to three, and adding a few hairs from each side with every cross-over. These are suited to slightly longer manes and

look smartest if secured with thread. Thin forelocks will benefit from a small French pleat even with a neck of normal plaits, as it will give the impression of thicker hair.

Horses with long manes can be plaited in a continuous French pleat, known as a **crest plait** when it is close to the top line of the neck, or an **Arab** or **native plait** when lower down. These are very quick to do and show off the neck very well, though they have the disadvantage of working loose easily, especially the

*Mane plaiting.*

77

*A neat ridge plait can look very impressive in the show ring.*

over, taking care to use equal sections and keeping the plait tight but not uncomfortably so. Having reached the end of the tail bone, the remaining section of hair is plaited to the end, doubled under itself and secured with thread or elastic bands. Having gone to the trouble of plaiting the tail, thread looks neater as it is less bulky and obvious.

All French pleats, whether they be on the mane or tail, can be done in two ways; in the true French style, where the sections are added from underneath, or in a **ridge plait** where they are taken over the top. French pleats have a woven appearance, whereas ridge plaits have a raised section of plait running from top to bottom. There is no question that neat and versatile plaiting is an art learned solely through experience. Practising long before an event will ensure deftness on the day and give peace of mind should a quick repair job be necessary. Ultimately, all forms of plaiting come down to personal preference, indeed some competitors do not plait at all. The style, amount of plaits, and means of securing should be decided by what looks best on the horse, not by fashion or helpful advice.

## CLIPPING

Working horses are clipped when their thick winter coat causes sweating and discomfort. The horse that is worked with a thick coat will take a long while to dry off following sweating, and may catch a chill as a result. The coat will also get clogged with dry sweat and be more difficult to clean.

Horses that are resting do not need clipping, as their coat is doing the primary job of maintaining body temperature. Horses in light work may not need clipping if their coat has been kept thin, by starting the rugging process early and adding a lightweight rug in early September so their full winter coat does not set and become woolly. The exact time of year the horse is clipped will depend on the climate, the work he is doing and the thickness

Arab versions. Three sections of hair are taken from the mane behind the ears and plaited, a small section added from one side at every cross over. If the hair is plaited directly on top of the neck in a true crest plait it can be taken from either side, which gives an impression of a good top line. For the best results they are plaited from directly above the neck, so are easiest to accomplish on small ponies or if sitting on the horse's back. Washing the mane even a week prior to using a long neck plait is asking for trouble. In fact the greasier the mane the better it will stay in place!

Tail plaits follow the same principle, and look impressive if done properly. Starting from the very top, a small amount of hair is added from each side of the tail at every cross

*Horses and ponies with thick winter coats may sweat excessively.*

of his coat, though usually the first clip is given in October. Second clips may be given in December or January if the coat has grown quickly and is inhibiting the horse's performance. Horses in very hard work may require clipping every month until January, when the hair growth slows down considerably. Certain animals are clipped throughout the year, generally the competition horses that are worked hard and frequently washed down, or show horses whose profile needs to be enhanced. Clipping is also administered to horses with parasitic complaints or skin infections, in order to clear the problem area and make treatment easier.

The most important factor to remember when planning the winter clip is the work that the horse is going to undertake. Clips should not be given just to improve appearance if the horse is in light work and could manage quite well without one. The style of clip seems too often decided by tradition rather than common sense, and the horse's workload and situation are given little thought. Protection is needed on the legs from mud, rain and brambles, and should only be clipped off when truly necessary. If this is removed, alternative protection should be provided in the field and when exercised by boots or bandages.

79

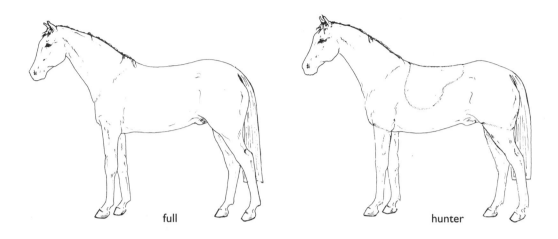

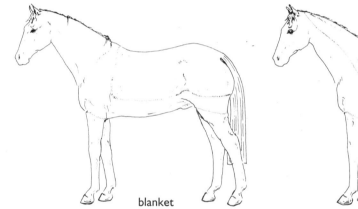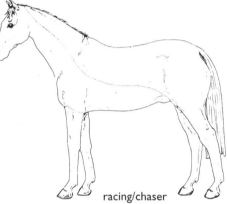

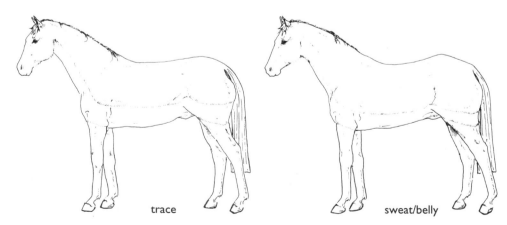

*Types of clip.*

## Types of Clip

There are several recognized styles of clip, designed with practicality and smartness in mind. Though most vary according to the horse and person clipping, they are used as guidelines by the majority of people.

Most of these clips can be varied a little to suit individual needs, in fact there is nothing to stop owners customizing a clip to suit a horse. Clipping upon advice or fashion may not be in the horse's best interest. What suits one horse may not suit another, and it is pointless to remove more hair than is necessary.

### Full Clip
With the full clip, the entire coat is removed, commonly used on stabled horses in continu-

ous hard work. Fully clipped horses will require plenty of artificial warmth from clothing, and are rarely turned out. If they are, additional protection, such as hoods and bandages, will be required. These horses will be prime candidates for chills and colds if not kept warm enough, or mud fever if their legs are not properly dried. The saddle area must be also be protected to prevent sores and rubbing, using a numnah or cushioned pad.

### Hunter Clip
Traditionally given to hunters, the saddle patch and legs are left unclipped for protection. The horse's own saddle or numnah is used as a template for the clip, the shape marked out prior to clipping with chalk. Both full and hunter clips leave the quarters bare,

*If the horse is to be worked, a low clip that removes the chest and belly hair will make him more comfortable.*

thus in my opinion making them both highly unsuitable for hunting! Hunters spend a good deal of time standing around in the cold, using up their energy in short bursts before standing around again. This is when the horse is most susceptible to chills, and requires some warmth around the quarters so the muscles do not seize up.

### Blanket Clip

The legs and back area are left unclipped, from just behind the withers to the tail, the clipping line along the side being level with the base of the saddle flap. This is a practical clip for horses in medium to hard work, as it allows protection to the legs and warmth around the quarters. A semi-circular patch is often left around the point of stifle where the hair changes direction – a small section may be clipped on either side of the tail to allow for sweating and ease of cleaning.

### Chaser, or Racing Clip

This is where the neck, head, belly and surrounding tail area are clipped, the clipping line running from the stifle to the top of the neck behind the ears. The line between the two points may be straight, or allow further hair coverage over the shoulder following the shape of the horse's body. Horses in medium to hard work will benefit from chaser clips.

### Trace Clip

This is similar to the blanket clip, except the line continues up the horse's neck, stopping at the jaw. Thus only the belly and neck hair is removed, allowing the horse in medium work to perform well and keep warm. High trace clips allow more hair to be removed, following the trace lines on a driving harness. They usually run above the point of stifle, leaving the semi-circular hair patch.

### Belly or Sweat Clip

This is commonly used on ponies or horses in light work, where the horse's belly and possibly the neck area are clipped.

## Clipping Equipment

There are several types of clipper available, suited to different workloads and parts of the body. The most common are electric hand clippers which are available in varying weights and motor sizes. They are practical to use, though some models may need turning off periodically to prevent overheating. Air-cooled versions, particularly the heavy-duty models, seem the best. Their disadvantages include the trailing cable and vibrating noise and some are louder than others, which may upset nervous horses.

Battery-operated clippers are practical and safe, the power being supplied in a rechargeable pack secured around the handler's waist.

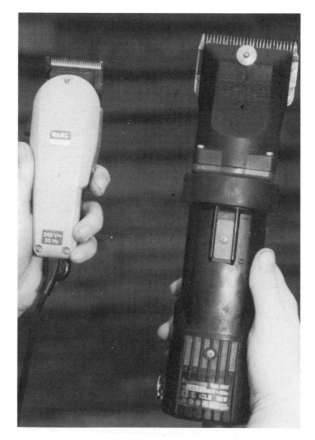

*Clippers are available in various weights and motor capacities.*

They are quiet, lightweight and can be used anywhere, and are particularly useful in places with limited access to power points. Battery-powered clippers are not heavy duty, and most have narrow blades, making them useful to clip difficult areas, especially around the head.

The smaller hand clippers are battery charged, for use around the head or on sensitive areas, and are extremely useful for nervous horses. Dog clippers may be used for the same purpose.

Old fashioned overhead clipping machines are mainly used in very large yards, and are designed to clip several horses in succession. They have large motors and are suspended from the roof of a clipping box.

## Preparation

The first consideration will be to decide who should clip the horse. Those fortunate enough to own their own clippers will not have a problem, but others will need to borrow a set or pay someone to come and clip the horse. Borrowing someone else's clippers is not advisable, unless some kind of official agreement has been made with regard to damage and insurance. No matter how careful horse owners are, accidents can happen and the clippers may be harmed, costing up to their original price to repair. It is much more advisable to book someone to come and clip the horse. These people usually offer a mobile service at a reasonable cost and will be quick and knowledgeable. It is always best to be totally honest when someone is coming to clip the horse, with regard to how the horse will react and what experiences he has had in the past. This may influence the time it takes to do the job, and will help enormously if the person clipping knows what to expect.

Horses not familiar with clippers should be gradually introduced, and the clippers run within the horse's earshot a few weeks prior to clipping. Alternatively, a tape recording of the clipper noise can be played if the clippers themselves are unavailable. Letting the horse feel the base of the clippers against his skin will also be an advantage, first turned off then and with the motor running.

Before clipping, the horse should be groomed to ensure no dirt interferes with the blades. If he is warm following light exercise, the pores will be open allowing easy hair removal, though he must not be hot or sweaty.

A 'clipping box' is very useful, particularly in bad weather. A large, airy box with a non-slip floor is preferable. Rubber matting gives good grip for both the horse and the person clipping, and also has insulating properties. The box should be well lit, as patches of hair can be missed under poor lighting conditions. Fluorescent strip lighting is particularly useful though expensive, and is actually preferable to natural sunlight as it creates no shadows. If a separate box is not available, alternatively a clean loose box or sheltered area outside will be suitable.

The horse's rugs should be at hand, so that as soon as he is clipped he can be rugged to prevent chilling. A body brush, curry-comb, and stable rubber to remove excess hair during and after clipping will also be useful as will a yard broom to tidy the area once the hair accumulates. Any restraining equipment, such as a twitch, should be kept nearby, though well out of harm's way so they are not trodden on. It is also best to have an assistant present when clipping, to hold and calm the horse, hold a foreleg so the clippers reach between the legs, or to restrain the horse if necessary. A haynet will keep the horse occupied, which is essential as a fidgety horse is impossible to clip properly.

Safety is of paramount importance, so rubber footwear must be worn by the persons involved at all times, and long hair tied back. A protective riding hat should also be worn at all times, although it is hot and cumbersome and best left to personal preference. Protective overalls are useful for both clipper and assistant, as the hair will get everywhere and be messy for all concerned. The horse's tail should be bandaged, and the mane kept out of

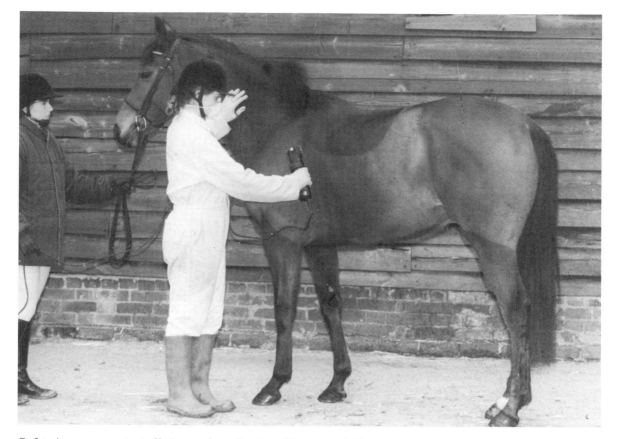

*Safety is paramount at all times when clipping. Most especially,*
*remember to keep the electric wire off the floor and out of harm's way.*

the way. Apart from being painful for the horse if the hair is tugged by the clippers, it will look unsightly and take a long time to grow back if a section is accidentally removed.

It is important to plan and assemble the necessary equipment beforehand to make the job of clipping as quick and trouble-free as possible. Having things close to hand will prevent the horse waiting around and chilling, and minimize boredom which induces fidgeting.

## Clipping Procedure

Assuming that the horse has been properly introduced to the sound and feel of the clippers, and that all the necessary equipment is to hand, proceed as follows:

1. After a thorough grooming, provide the horse with something to occupy him (such as a haynet). Tie him up or have him held still by an assistant.

2. Mark out the desired clip line with white chalk, or coloured chalk on lighter horses such as greys. Saddle soap can be used but leaves a greasy residue, and is not easily seen.

3. Run the clippers to remind the horse of their sound and feel. The shoulder is the best place to start as it is a flat area and not too sensitive. Place the clippers on the area to be clipped and, keeping the blades flat, go against the lie of the coat in long sweeping strokes with an even pressure. Continue until the body area is completed.

4. Clip between the legs. As the skin wrinkles

and is easily cut here, the assistant should hold one of the horse's forelegs forward while you clip this area. The assistant can also lift his head when clipping the neck and around the jaw, so the skin lays flat.

5. Continue clipping in this manner until all the areas are complete. Leave a triangle of hair around the sheath, as this is a sensitive area some horses find very ticklish; great care should be taken around delicate areas such as this in case the horse kicks out.

6. Clean and oil the clippers.

The clippers should be cleaned and oiled at regular intervals, and turned off if they show signs of overheating. At this point a rug should be put over the horse to prevent chilling. When the clip is complete and level on both sides, the horse should be quickly brushed and wiped over, and then rugged up.

## Restraining

Some horses find the whole business of clipping a ticklish or alarming experience, and may need restraining. If they are just fidgeting, holding up a foreleg or pinching a section of skin on the neck may have the desired effect. Skin pinching releases a small amount of natural sedatives called endorphins from the brain, which has a minimal calming effect. Twitches are the most effective restraining method, and work by pinching the upper lip below the nostril, releasing a large amount of endorphins and relaxing the horse. The traditional home-made twitch is a length of looped twine attached to a solid handle – the twine is placed around the upper lip and the handle twisted, so the loop gets smaller and pinches. Thin twine may restrict the blood flow too

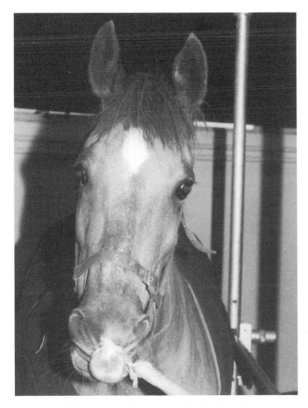

*A correctly fitted traditional twitch, fused to restrain a horse.*

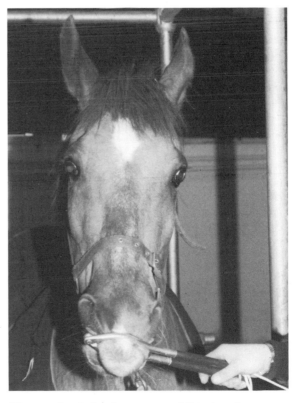

*'Humane' twitches have a metal 'loop' and are simple and practical to use.*

85

much or even damage the skin, so should not be used. Manufactured twitches are much easier to administer, and close around the nose in an action similar to a pair of nutcrackers. They are then secured and either held by the assistant or attached to the headcollar. When applied properly, twitches are usually successful, though should not be left on for long periods of time. Both should be used by an experienced person and taken off as soon as possible, then the nose immediately rubbed to stimulate blood flow.

If the horse requires further restraint, it is safest to have a veterinary surgeon sedate him. This must be booked in advance, and the vet should supervise the first few minutes of sedation to ensure the horse reacts favourably to the drug. The horse's feeding schedule may need to be rearranged as the drugs' absorption may be affected by what has been consumed. The majority of awkward horses who are sedated can be clipped, though some seem able to fight the drugs. In these cases veterinary advice must be sought, as this is a dangerous situation which can result in human or equine injury. The horse may throw himself around, not being fully in control of his movements. A last resort is to have the horse transported to the veterinary surgery where he can be completely sedated and clipped. The practise is time consuming, impractical and very expensive, and should only take place when in the veterinary surgeon's opinion there is no other option.

## Care of the Horse after Clipping

Most importantly, after clipping the horse should be kept warm as the initial loss of coat will come as a bit of a shock. The type of rug to use will depend on the time of year, but should allow for the addition of further rugs should the weather turn very cold. A rough guide is to fit a thin sheet (a bed sheet will be quite suitable) under a thick nightrug for the first clip, which will provide an insulating layer and also protect the rug from dirt and grease. One or two blankets can be fitted underneath when the weather gets worse, so by mid-winter the horse may have three or four layers on, depending on his clip and breeding. Woollen blankets should lie between the sheet and the rug, as the fibres may irritate the skin. For the fully clipped horse, stable bandages may be necessary in very cold weather, and should be worn loose over padding with no pressure to the legs.

It is unwise to turn the horse out straight after clipping, as he will need time to adjust to the feeling and adapt his body temperature. However, when he does go out he will need a warm New Zealand or turn-out rug, fitted over an under-rug in cold weather. Hoods will also be beneficial both in the field and stable, though are only necessary for the horse with head and neck clipped out. A woollen or waterproof exercise sheet will also be useful in the cold or wet weather, to protect the loins and keep the muscles warm.

## Care of the Clippers

Clippers must be kept in good working order, brushed and oiled during and after use and cleaned regularly. The dirt and hair can get inside the air filter, which should be dismantled and brushed out according to the manufacturer's instructions. The blades should be sharpened and changed on a regular basis, as clipping with blunt blades will pull at the hair and give an uneven clip. Servicing should be carried out by the manufacturer or their recommended company, as the warranty may not be applicable if other agents have carried out repair work. The clippers should then be stored in a warm, dry environment, in safe working order for the following season.

## Additional Use of the Clippers

*Hogging*
Hogging is complete removal of the mane, usually for appearance to enhance the profile of a thickset, cobby horse. Hogged manes

require minimal daily maintenance, and need shortening approximately every month throughout the year. When hogging a long mane, it is easiest to remove excess hair with scissors first, then with an assistant holding the head so the neck is outstretched, clip along the crest from withers to poll. It will be necessary to stand on something solid such as a crate to get an even line, particularly on larger horses, and to check the profile from either side of the neck.

*Tidying Legs and Feet*
Throughout the year excess hair around the lower legs can be clipped off to enhance their shape. For best results this should be done carefully with lightweight trimmers as the hair should not be taken from close to the leg. The line around the coronet band of the foot can also be carefully clipped with trimmers to enhance the feet, though usually done only for showing purposes. Excess removal of the hair around the foot can cause the horn to become soggy, as the hair drains water away in bad weather. Normal clippers will be too clumsy

for these delicate areas, and may remove too much hair at once leaving an untidy line. If in doubt, use scissors!

*Exposing*
When horses are freezemarked for security reasons in some cases the surrounding hair will need shaving. On dark horses, the freezemark shows up as white hair, but on greys and lighter horses the freezemark shows up as bald skin. In the winter the coat may disguise the mark, and one careful stroke of the clippers is necessary for it to be visible.

---

ECONOMIZE

- When grooming, use unscented moist wipes for the face and dock. This will save time and is more hygienic than using sponges.
- Tea towels or fabric beer mats make good stable rubbers.
- Using a brush attachment on the hose when bathing will speed up the rinsing process and reduce the amount of water used.

---

# 6 The Horse's Health

As the horse's good health is of prime importance to every owner, it is vital to have two things; a rudimentary knowledge of ailments and disorders, and a very good vet! The subject of equine health is vast and complicated, and discussed fully in specialist books. Therefore, this chapter looks briefly at the most common ailments, and veterinary and alternative treatments. For in-depth knowledge, it is advisable to refer to a comprehensive veterinary manual. All reading must be complemented by sensible horse management, and includes taking veterinary advice if in any doubt concerning the horse's health.

*The horse's health should be of prime importance: a horse in poor condition reflects badly on his owner.*

It has been discussed in Chapter 1 that the horse must be treated as an individual and his own characteristics taken into account. Owners who do know their horses and take care to provide them with a healthy, low-risk environment are already preventing some ailments. By observing the signs of good health and following the routine procedures discussed in Chapters 1 and 2 respectively, owners will be doing their utmost. However ill-health does occur, and must be diagnosed and treated as soon as possible.

## COMMON AILMENTS AND INJURIES

### Colic

Colic is a digestive disorder, and the term is used to describe a range of abdominal pains similar in essence to indigestion in humans. It can range from a slight stomach ache to a life-threatening illness, though most cases are not serious and are easily treated. The horse with the first stages of colic may be restless and off his food, perhaps pawing the ground, pacing the box or kicking the walls. As the pain increases he may lie down and stare at his belly, then attempt to roll and become nervous. The temperature, pulse and respiration rates will also increase. This is particularly noticeable in the breathing which may appear quite shallow, and the high temperature which often induces sweating.

There are several classifications of the disorder: **impacted colic**, which is connected to the diet, for instance, the feeding regime may have been altered, an excess amount of water consumed after food, or excess work undertaken following food; **sand colic**, where sediment from the drinking supply is consumed along with the water (this should not occur when a suitable water supply is provided); **flatulent colic**, where excess gases are caught up in the gut and press against the wall. Horses that windsuck may induce

flatulent colic, as may those with food fermenting in the gut. Lastly and most commonly, **spasmodic colic** occurs when the intestine goes into spasms, the causes of which can include any of those listed above. Horses with heavy worm burdens may experience colic following worming. The parasites may cause a blockage as they are expelled, or may affect the bloodstream to the gut while they live off the horse prior to worming.

There are two schools of thought with regard to treating colic. One (which I am inclined to agree with) insists that the vet is called almost immediately, if after about half an hour the symptoms are the same or have worsened. The horse should be kept warm with a rug, and his food and water removed; he should be left well alone, and not given any concoctions or treatments prior to the vet's arrival.

The opposing view veers more towards treatment by the owner, including walking the horse in-hand to prevent the horse from getting down and rolling. This behaviour may cause a twisted gut, a condition that is almost always fatal and occurs when the membrane supporting the gut is torn, and this could happen during particularly violent rolling. Laxative bran mashes or drenches containing kaolin, liquid paraffin or homoeopathic ingredients are also sometimes given, but rarely on veterinary advice; a bran mash may worsen the blockage if too dry, and in any case will taste bland to the poor horse who is off his food; the drench could easily go down the windpipe if not properly administered, causing further problems. However, I must say that I do know of two experienced owners whose horses are prone to mild colic, and on seeing the initial colic symptoms give the horse a syringe of liquid paraffin which appears to do the trick. Whilst this seems to work for them, it is certainly not to be advised, particularly as a strong purgative drench may cause, in addition to the desired bowel action, tearing of the gut membrane as the blockage moves.

My own advice would be to monitor the colic for a short amount of time. If the horse does not become agitated and looks only a little off colour, the colic may well pass within the hour. If he becomes nervous, breaks out in sweat or attempts to roll, call the vet and keep him as calm as possible.

## Colds and Coughs

The equine cold is very similar to that of the human, and is usually caused by excess exposure to the cold air or another horse with a respiratory infection. The initial symptoms are a runny eyes and nose, with a clear to yellow discharge and dull coat. The horse may also be off his food and show signs of being cold, even though his temperature and pulse may increase. If colds are treated at this stage they are usually harmless, but if ignored they can quickly develop in to an infection, bad cough or respiratory disease. A slight cough often accompanies a cold, though it will range in severity. Any coughing is potentially dangerous to the system, and if persistent must be treated by the vet. Since infectious viruses are very easily passed by coughing, it is best to isolate the affected horse.

The treatment is to rest the horse, as working him may damage the respiratory system. He must be kept warm, but must also be given plenty of fresh air and ventilation. If he is normally turned out, then providing he is well rugged up he can still do so. It is a good idea to soak or steam the hay until he has recovered, or feed him vacuum-packed hay so that the dust particles do not irritate him. As with humans, there are a number of remedies available to owners, from pharmaceutical drugs to homoeopathic remedies. A slight cold or cough will disappear quickly when the correct procedures are followed. If it doesn't, it may indicate signs of an infection and could lead to serious diseases such as pneumonia. If in any doubt the vet should be called, in order to administer drugs and advise on further treatment. It is always important to remember that horses in poor condition will have low immunity to disease, especially if their respiratory system has been damaged before. They will require immediate veterinary examination.

## Chronic Obstructive Pulmonary Disease (COPD)

If calling the vet for a cold seems unnecessary, one only has to look at a horse with COPD to see that it is not. Also known as *broken wind*, this is a serious respiratory condition that can follow an untreated cold or cough, damaging the airways and lungs and possibly affecting the horse's working life. The horse with COPD will have alarming reactions to dust spores, including a bad cough, runny nose and difficulty in breathing. Dust-free hay and bedding is essential, and regular visits from the vet. Though there are many drugs available nowadays that successfully treat COPD, the horse with severely damaged airways may need a permanent course of drugs, dust-free environment, and restricted exercise. One of the most common drugs is a powdered bronchodilator, which dilates the tissues and membranes of the airways that are reacting to the dust spores. The drug must be used in conjunction with the clean air management routine or it will have little effect. On no account should the horse be worked until in the vet's opinion he is well enough, as this will damage the lungs further.

Nursing the horse with broken wind is a long process, as he will need a long rest from work and a strict management programme. Though for some horses COPD can mean the end of their career, as any work aggravates their susceptible respiratory system, fortunately these cases are few and far between. Good management often prevents the condition occurring, or successfully controls it so the horse can lead a relatively normal life. Veterinary advice really is important, as the severity of the condition may not be apparent until it is too late.

## Strangles

Strangles is an infectious respiratory disease, passed on via infected horses, environment or equipment. Symptoms include a high temperature, loss of appetite, a thick, yellow nasal discharge and enlarged glands under the jaw, which may form abscesses and burst. Treatment is to call the vet who may administer antibiotics or anti-inflammatory drugs. Food should be of a sloppy consistency and easy to swallow and, most important of all, the horse should be isolated and stringent hygiene procedures followed to prevent the disease spreading to other horses. This involves wearing protective clothing retained for use around the sick horse, disinfecting boots when leaving his box, using separate feeding utensils, and burning bedding and any swabs taken from the nostrils. The horse must be allowed plenty of time to recuperate following the disease, and should only be removed from isolation when the vet does not consider other horses to be at risk. This may be a further month after the abscesses have burst, and hygiene procedures must be continued during this time.

## Lameness

The term lameness covers an alarmingly large number of complaints, often difficult to diagnose and trace to a particular cause. Though most symptoms of lameness appear in the limbs, they can be traced to other parts of the

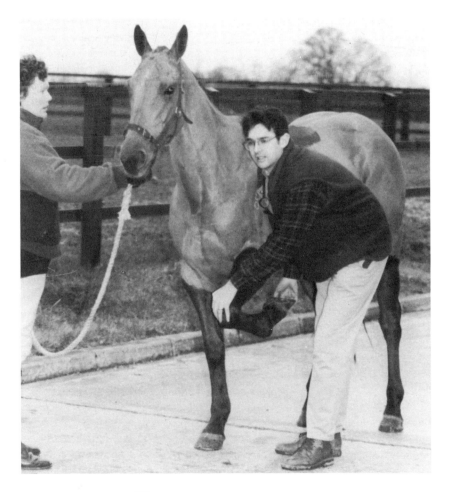

*The vet may carry out various tests for lameness.*

91

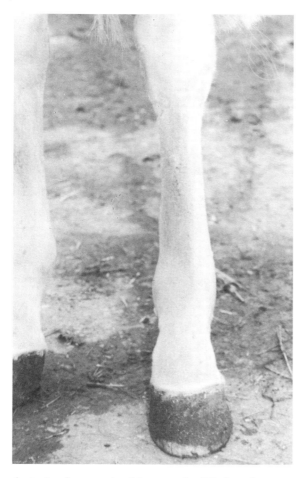

*A strained or sprained leg may be filled and swollen.*

defects and diseases of the joints and bones may cause similar symptoms, and can be diagnosed by a vet following long-term or persistent lameness.

Strains and sprains will be characterized by heat and swelling, and are treated with cold therapies to reduce tenderness. The most basic treatment is to hose the area gently with cold running water, though there are a number of less time-consuming methods. These include aqua boots that fill with water and produce a jacuzzi effect; gel sachets that are refrigerated then bandaged to the leg, and cooling boots and bandages containing crystals that melt against the leg following refrigeration. There are also various cooling gels and pastes that are applied to the leg which work in the same way. A useful home-made alternative is to soak gamgee in diluted witch-hazel or water, then bandage it to the leg. The gamgee can also be frozen prior to dressing, having been moulded to the shape of the leg. Ultra-sound treatment is often used on serious strain injuries, and can reduce muscle spasm, increase blood flow and improve the elasticity of blood flow. It can also be used successfully to treat bone damage, and although there are several machines available to the general public, it is strongly advised that a qualified practitioner administers any ultra-sound treatment.

Stiffness and bruising can be treated with heat, which dilates blood vessels thus increasing blood flow to the area, and reduces pain. Treatment includes infra-red and ultra-violet heat lamps; compresses (soaked towels or gamgee at blood temperature) bandaged with an even pressure over the area, mud packs applied as a paste under bandages, and liquid arnica massaged into the area.

Good old-fashioned rest is one of the best therapies for lameness, though if following several days rest and treatment minor lameness has not gone away, the vet should be called in order to administer anti-inflammatory drugs, or advise investigatory treatment and X-rays, or physiotherapy.

body such as the back and shoulders – therefore lameness should not be thought of solely as a condition of the leg. The lame horse will be in a certain amount of pain, though the extent will differ according to the condition and sensitivity of the horse. Symptoms include stiffness during movement or at rest, restricted action and swollen or hardened areas.

The two most common causes of minor lameness are direct trauma from an injury, such as a kick or a stumble in the field, or excessive strain, for example from carrying a heavy rider or absorbing concussion from hard ground. Hereditary disorders, conformation

## Laminitis

Laminitis, or 'founder' is a serious disease, commonly caused by excessive amounts of carbohydrate in the diet leading to impaired blood supply to the feet. The sensitive laminae within the foot becomes inflamed, and starts to come away from the insensitive laminae. In serious cases, they may separate, and the pedal bone within the foot may rotate and press on the sole. Laminitis normally occurs in the forefeet and is very painful as the laminae will be inflamed but unable to swell within the hoof.

The symptoms of laminitis in the first stages may be a restricted, pottery action, with some heat in the foot. When the feet are trimmed or shod, the white line of horn visible on the underside of the foot may be blurred and a little soft. The horse may also show discomfort when he is shod. Horses with serious laminitis have a typical leaning back stance, to take the weight off the forefeet. They will be unwilling to move, and may lie down to alleviate the pain.

Therapy can be effective if the disease is treated immediately. The first thing to do is stop working the horse, restrict his grazing and cut down the diet to just roughage. The vet should be called immediately, and may prescribe anti-inflammatory drugs and arrange X-rays to determine the extent of the damage. One of the most distressing treatments the owner may have to administer is enforced walking, which may be painful for the horse but improves the circulation. However, this is only advised in the cases where the pedal bones are stable, as movement may cause damage in serious cases. In the short term, cold hosing may also be beneficial and, in the long term, a revised diet plan and corrective shoeing programme, advised by the veterinary surgeon and farrier respectively. Cell therapy may be given once the horse is on the road to recovery, which involves replacing damaged cells with healthy ones. It is administered by a cell-therapy practitioner following veterinary advice.

Laminitis can be fatal if the pedal bone is left unsupported and drops down to the sole. In these cases there is rarely anything that can be done for the horse, but if the disease is diagnosed in its early stages it is unlikely to progress this far. Once a horse has recovered from laminitis he will be susceptible to it again, and his diet should be worked out accordingly following veterinary advice. This will also mean restricting the grazing, particularly in the spring when the grass is lush. The symptoms can reappear alarmingly quickly if the horse has access to too much grass. Horses that have previously been affected by the disease may have small ridges of horn on their hooves, caused by impaired blood supply and subsequent impaired growth.

## Azoturia

This condition is also known as 'Monday morning disease' as it often occurs after a rest period. The cause of the disease is continually being researched, though the traditional theory states that a build-up of lactic acid occurs in the muscles when excessive concentrates are fed in conjunction with a lack of exercise. This in turn means the circulatory system is not stimulated sufficiently to remove the build-up, so it stays around the muscles of the loins and hindquarters. In addition to this cause there may be hereditary factors, as certain horses seem more prone than others, and deficiencies within the blood stream caused by mineral or electrolyte imbalances.

The symptoms appear suddenly as cramps in the hindquarters, soon after the horse has begun work. He may stagger or even fall over, and he will be distressed and in pain. If azoturia is suspected, call the vet immediately. The horse should not be moved unless there is no other option and, even then, very slowly to prevent muscle damage. He should be kept warm and calm until the vet arrives. Prevention is important, so the diet should be modified according to work, and the amount of concentrate feeds lowered before a rest period.

## Ringworm

This is a highly contagious skin disease, caused by a fungus passed on by other horses or humans, or by an affected environment or equipment. The symptoms are raised circular patches of hair which may appear all over the body, leading to hair loss and scabs. Veterinary attention is important. The vet will prescribe a fungicidal treatment which is administered directly to the affected area, usually in the form of a wash or ointment. Fastidious hygiene is important, so all equipment should be disinfected, and the owner must wear protective gloves which should be discarded after contact with the horse. Premises should be disinfected too, as the fungus can lie dormant for years, particularly in wooden stables, which are harder to clean thoroughly. An unfortunate side-effect of the disease is the disfiguring hair growth that may occur every year, following the same pattern as the original hair loss.

## Wounds

Wounds can be classified into five categories:
- **Incision** – a clean-cut injury in the form of a slash, caused by sharp cutting objects such as blades or glass.
- **Laceration**: an untidy rip to the flesh, caused by sharp tearing objects such as barbed wire.
- **Puncture**: a deep hole in the flesh caused by long objects such as nails or stakes. Smaller puncture wounds can be caused by thorns and brambles.
- **Bruise**: an area of flesh with unbroken skin over broken blood vessels, caused by blows or kicks.
- **Self-inflicted injury**: these often occur through faulty action or conformation. *Over-reaching*, where the hind toes cut in to the heels of the fore feet, can be prevented with over-reach boots. Brushing, where both fore or hind legs brush or knock against one another, can be prevented with

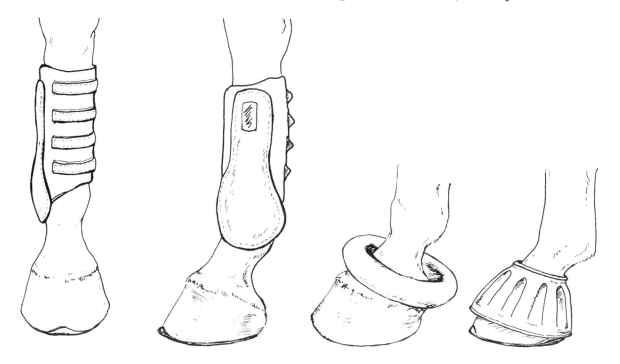

*Boots to prevent self-inflicted injury.*

brushing boots. *Capped elbows* are sore areas at the point of elbow caused by a lack of bedding. Fitting a sausage boot around the fetlock so the shoe does not come in to contact with the elbow, and providing thick bedding will alleviate the problem.

The majority of wounds can be avoided by careful management, such as checking fields for damaged fencing and discarded rubbish. It is alarming what can be unearthed in some fields, such as rusty objects that have been in the ground for years. The yard must also be checked regularly. Splinters from the stable may also appear from time to time, and nails from the farrier's visits can easily get lost. However, no matter how vigilant owners are accidents always happen, and wounds must be carefully treated to prevent infection setting in.

The first thing to do is stop the bleeding. Minor wounds stop by themselves, though more serious wounds may need to be held at the sides or pressed with something flat such as the thumb. Cold hosing will restrict the blood vessels and may help, though veterinary treatment must be summoned immediately if the wound does not stop bleeding. No medication should be applied prior to the vet's arrival as it may interfere with treatment. The vet may stitch the area which will assist in the healing process and may leave a minor scar. Proud flesh (granulated tissue) may form otherwise, which looks unsightly and may be covering un-healed flesh beneath. The vet will give advice on further treatment, and may prescribe antibiotics.

Puncture wounds will need special monitoring, as they may look minor but in fact be quite deep. There is a danger of the outer layer of flesh healing over the wound, trapping infection inside. If the wound is minor it can be cleansed daily and the outer scab taken off, however serious wounds must not be interfered with, and veterinary advice must be sought as stitching or surgery may be required.

If the wound is minor it can be dressed without calling the vet. It should be cleansed with warm, slightly salty water, using clean cotton wool. Wash your hands first to prevent the spread of infection. Antiseptic spray, ointment or powder can then be applied in moderation when the wound is dry, though it must have access to fresh air to heal properly. Manufactured wound dressings are available and can be applied over dry or wet wounds, allowing freedom of movement and forming an antiseptic barrier. The ingredients penetrate beneath the damaged tissue, protecting the lower healthy tissue from infection, and lowering the risk of proud flesh.

## Mud Fever and Rain Scald

These are skin irritations caused by the same bacteria, and occur on the legs and back respectively. Germs get underneath the skin and lie beneath small scabs causing the hair to appear tufty and the skin bumpy. The bacteria seem more common in certain soils, though generally occur when the skin is exposed to excess moisture and mud and is not dried off properly. It can also occur when the horse sweats beneath rugs or boots where the bacteria are present. Prevention of mud fever is to wash any mud off the legs before drying thoroughly. Leaving it to dry before brushing could drive dirt particles into the legs, as the skin is quite tender. Horses that have contracted it will need their legs bathed and the scabs removed, then the legs should be carefully dried and treated daily with antibiotic medication obtained from the vet.

Prevention of rainscald is more difficult as it affects the back. The horse must be dried off if he gets wet and never put rugs or tack on damp or sweaty areas. When treating rainscald, saddles should not be used on the affected area which should be kept as free as possible from moisture and sweat. This may involve keeping the horse in the stable during wet weather, as rugging him up out-doors will aggravate the condition. If he does get wet he should be dried off thoroughly. The same medication is used as with mud fever, and the scabs removed so the antibiotics can kill off the bacteria.

## Cracked Heels

Cracked heels are painful sores or open wounds at the heel. They are caused by the area becoming wet and not being dried off properly, and commonly occur following bathing or standing in wet bedding. The horse can go lame as movement is very painful.

To help prevent cracked heels owners should always dry the horse's legs off, paying particular attention to the heels. Horses with clipped fetlock hair are more susceptible, as the hair acts as drainage when the leg is wet. A layer of petroleum jelly can be applied to the area prior to exercise, turn out or bathing to prevent moisture gathering at the heel.

Cracked heels should be bathed as for a normal wound, and medicated ointment applied. This will help to soften the skin, as sprays and powders may dry out the area, allowing the heels to crack further. When the wounds begin to heal the skin can be kept soft with petroleum jelly.

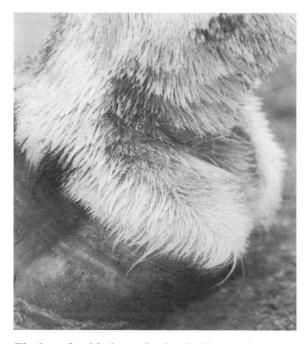

*The legs should always be dried off properly to prevent cracked heels.*

## Sweet Itch

This is an allergic reaction, the exact cause being uncertain. The most common theory is an allergy to midge bites during the spring and autumn which may be aggravated even more by sunlight. Some horses are more prone to sweet itch than others and ponies more often still. It affects the mane and tail, which can be rubbed raw by the horse to alleviate the discomfort.

For animals prone to the condition, prevention entails keeping them stabled in the early morning and evening when the midges are at their worst. Treatment comes in the form of sweet itch compounds and washes from saddlers or veterinary surgeries, anti-inflammatory drugs and fly repellents. A course of B-vitamins (usually given in injections) may keep the midges at bay, and stabling the horse during intense sunlight will bring relief.

## Thrush

This is a fungal infection of the tissue around the frog within the foot, caused by prolonged contact with dirty, wet ground. The frog itself may go soft and disintegrate, and is usually accompanied by a foul smell. In severe cases the horse may go lame. The two main causes of thrush are dirty bedding (particularly deep litter) and muddy fields. Any situation where the horse's feet are in continual contact with excess dirt and moisture can induce thrush.

The best way to prevent the infection is to provide a hygienic environment, regularly pick out the feet, muck out properly and provide plenty of clean bedding. It may also be necessary to put straw down in the field over muddy patches, particularly by the gate where the horse may wait to come in. Following treatment by the farrier to pare away diseased horn, the foot should be cleaned thoroughly before applying antiseptic or astringent medication to the area — copper-sulphate crystals or hydrogen peroxide are commonly used, though owners should check with the vet first to see what he advises.

## Sunburn

Sunburn is a natural reaction to sunlight affecting non-pigmented (pink) skin, usually around the muzzle. The area becomes slightly inflamed, and may develop scabby patches which can become infected. Once the sunburn has got to this stage, an antibacterial ointment containing a sunscreen should be applied. As a form of prevention, human sunscreen works well, or stabling badly affected animals on sunny days.

# THE FIRST AID KIT

It is important to have a supply of first aid equipment at the yard which is kept stocked up at all times. The basic kit should consist of:
- Veterinary thermometer.
- Antiseptic solution or salt, to add to water when bathing wounds.
- Clean cotton wool to bathe wounds.
- Antiseptic ointment, spray and wound powder to dress the wound following bathing.
- Gauze, lint and non-stick dressing for wounds.
- Surgical or elastoplast tape to hold dressings in place.
- Gamgee to protect wounds under bandages.
- Clean surgical bandages to hold the dressing in place.
- Round-ended scissors for cutting dressings.
- Animalintex poultice.
- Witch hazel to bathe minor wounds or reduce inflammation.
- Tweezers for removing thorns.
- Fly repellent to protect wounds.
- Petroleum jelly to soften skin as wound is healing.
- Skin regeneration cream for serious wounds.
- Small, clean bucket to hold water.

Additional treatments such as cooling gels and ice packs should be kept refrigerated ready for use, and easily accessible in an emergency. The horse's personal file including veterinary records, vaccination, worming and shoeing dates should be kept nearby, as should the vet's telephone number. He can advise on any additional items deemed necessary, and provide owners with any treatment unobtainable from saddlers. It is most convenient to keep the items in a portable box or container that can be taken to the horse when necessary, rather than taking items a few at a time from a chest or cabinet.

---

**TRAVELLING**

Preparing a small travelling first aid kit to take to shows or events is useful. It should be stored in a container that can double up as a bucket, and should contain:
- Antiseptic solution or salt.
- Unscented moist wipes in case there is no water supply.
- Cotton wool.
- Antiseptic medication (ointment, spray or powder).
- Gauze, lint and non-stick dressing.
- Surgical tape.
- Gamgee and surgical bandage.
- Scissors and tweezers.
- The vet's telephone number.

---

# NURSING

The very sick horse will need attention throughout the day, even though this may be impractical for owners who work or have families. There must be someone available, if not the owner then a reliable friend, to monitor his temperature, pulse and respiration, check on him regularly and carry out veterinary instructions. If at all possible the horse should be isolated, particularly if his illness is contagious or infectious. As with ill humans, the horse will not be too bothered by his surroundings, and will not appreciate the fuss and bustle of a busy environment. He should have comfortable, warm clothing, and the stable should be draught free and clean. If he is able to leave the stable for in-hand walking and grazing, he may be taken out for around ten minutes twice a day, with his stable bandages left on. His feeding levels should be

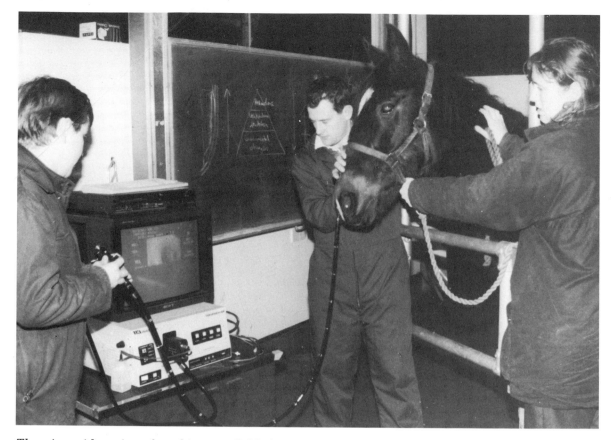

*There is a wide variety of machines available for monitoring and assessment of a horse's health and condition, and for providing treatment when appropriate. Here, an endoscope is being used to examine the stomach.*

adjusted as he will not be working, and he may be off his food. Palatable, easily digestive foods will be appreciated, with some succulents to tempt him.

## Exercising the Sick Horse

If the horse is not seriously ill or only has minor injuries, the vet may advise that he is exercised. In fact in the case of leg injuries it may be imperative the horse moves about to prevent the legs filling, to aid circulation and encourage blood flow to the area. This may be a better option than turning the horse out in some cases, as he could race around the field unsupervised and cause further damage.

There are no hard and fast guidelines to exercising the sick horse, which is why veterinary advice must be sought according to which area is injured or ailing. It is important not to aggravate the injured part of the body. For example, exertion on the lungs of a horse with COPD will worsen the problem, and work on hard ground may cause concussion to strained or injured legs. If the horse is allowed to do a little light work, he can be ridden at the walk for around ten to fifteen minutes once or twice a day. This is enough to get the circulation going, and make the unfit muscles work gently but not strain themselves. If the horse is to be nursed for several weeks the walking exercise can be lengthened from twenty to thirty minutes, using transitions and a few school movements. It is not necessary to trot and canter the horse as he will use up energy very quickly using fuel to fight disease or regenerate tissue. Walking is quite sufficient and uses more of the muscles at any one time, so a certain area will not be weaker when it comes to fittening. It is very important to keep the horse ticking over but not push him too far, as this will delay the healing process and tire him out.

Once the sick horse has fully recovered, particularly if he has had a long period off proper work, he will have lost some of his suppleness, and probably be lacking in balance. His immune system may be low and susceptible to further illness, so he must be fittened slowly. His walking work should continue, gradually increasing to include trot and canter, with lots of transitions and school movements. This will improve his balance and flexibility, and slowly rebuild the weakened muscle. When he is ready, a little gymnastic jumping and grid-work will help to bring him back in to fitness. All rehabilitation exercise should be done on the advice of the vet.

## METHODS OF THERAPY

Fortunately there are many methods of therapy available today to treat an ailing horse, from home remedies to alternative treatments. This section covers some of the most common methods.

### Traditional Treatments

*Poulticing*
Hot poultices are used to stimulate the blood supply to a certain area, and to help repair damaged tissue through the application of heat. They are also used to draw out infection and bruising. The most popular poultice available is *Animalintex*, an impregnated piece of padding and gauze which is soaked in boiling water. When it has cooled to blood tempera-ture, the padding is placed over the affected area and bandaged in place. The advantages of Animalintex are that it can be cut to the exact size, and infection or foreign bodies drawn from the area are visible on the padding following removal.

**Kaolin poultices** Effective but impractical. A tin of kaolin is placed in a pan of boiling water, then the warm paste is smeared on a section of lint and covered with polythene. A piece of gamgee is then placed over the top before a bandage is applied to hold the dress-ing in place. Kaolin poultices retain heat well and are useful for reducing swelling, but messy and time consuming to use.

**Comfrey poultices** Similar to kaolin poul-tices, these are prepared by soaking cut com-frey leaves in boiling water before applying them to a strip of lint covered with gauze, with gamgee over the top and a bandage to hold the dressing in place.

**Bran poultices** are commonly used for poul-ticing wounded or sore feet. Boiling water and antiseptic are poured on to the bran until it is crumbly, then once it has cooled to blood tem-perature it is placed within a polythene bag which fits over the foot. There are several means of securing the dressing: plaster ban-dage or a hessian sack secured at the top, fol-lowed by a surgical bandage will suffice, though poultice boots are much more practi-cal. They are made from leather or rubber, and hold the dressing well, preventing the bag from splitting and dirt getting to the wound.

**Cold compresses** These can be used in a sim-ilar way as poultices to draw out heat, using an inner cloth soaked in cold water followed by a thick outer cloth. A piece of gamgee is added over the top, and then the dressing ban-daged in place. Additives such as clay paste, arnica or witch hazel can be added to the first layer, though these should be used beneath linen cloth or gauze.

Poultices should never be used over a joint, as there is a danger of drawing out precious joint oil, and they should be renewed at least every twelve hours.

## Fomentations

These follow the same principles as poulticing, and are used to apply heat to areas difficult to poultice. Thick towels or flannels are soaked in hot water and cooled to blood temperature, and applied for a few minutes to the affected area. They can be left on, if there is a means of securing them, but are usually changed frequently and the process repeated.

## Tubbing

Tubbing is a method of immersing the feet or lower limbs in warm water, using a non-metal bucket or container. The process is commonly used for bruises or punctures to the sole. The leg is placed in the bucket for around twenty minutes, and repeated several times a day. Some horses may panic and kick the bucket over, so there must be someone present at all times. The limbs should be allowed to dry naturally or with gentle rubbing using a towel, paying particular attention to the heels so they do not crack.

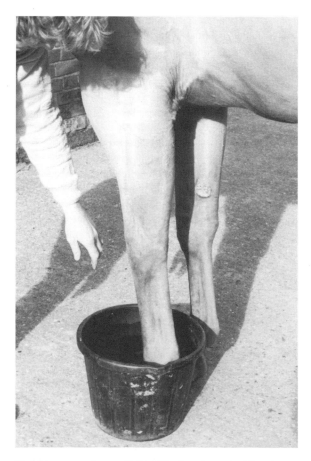

*Tubbing may be useful in the treatment of bruises and sole punctures.*

## Cold Hosing

This is an excellent method of cooling an area and reducing inflammation. Rather than just pointing the hose at the affected area, hold the end pointing upwards so the water will envelope the area rather than spray at a certain point. This will be more beneficial as it will cool a larger area. Owners should make sure the limbs are dried off, but avoid rubbing with a towel as this will create heat.

## Firing

Firing is an old-fashioned form of heat treatment, whereby hot irons are applied to the leg to cause an inflammatory reaction and subsequent tissue healing. Quite apart from the fact there is little circumstantial evidence in favour of firing – and even this is very subjective – the process is inhumane and in the modern world of technological wizardry, totally unnecessary.

# Contemporary Treatments

## Physiotherapy

Physiotherapy is used to assist natural healing within damaged tissues, helping the site of injury return to normal and function properly, and assisting in pain relief.

## Cold Treatments

Aqua boots are a practical alternative to cold hosing and use up less water. They are fitted to the leg and filled with water, and using a compressor attachment which aggravates the water to produce a jacuzzi effect, they give the leg a pleasurable hydrotherapy treatment. They are used for up to twenty minutes at a time, several times a day.

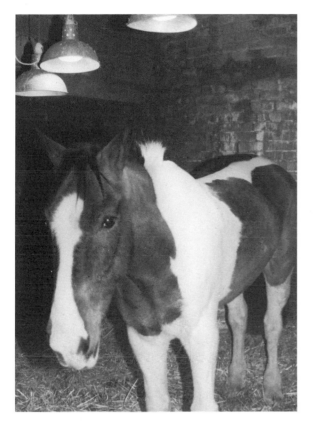

*Heat therapy is useful for relieving pain and repairing tissue.*

### Heat Treatments

There are several different methods of applying heat to the body, in order to ease pain and inflammation and encourage the repair of damaged tissue. Superficial heat in the form of infra-red and ultra violet lamps (to recreate heat and sunlight respectively) is used to supply energy to the two layers of skin, producing a rise in both temperature and circulation, and consequently dilation of blood vessels. Larger yards may have purpose-built solariums with a set of lights within cradles, though they are widely available on a smaller scale at a reasonable price. Exposure times will be listed in the manufacturer's instructions. Hot and cold therapy, or contrast bathing, can be used to cause constriction and dilation of blood vessels. This is done by applying alternate hot and ice cold towels to the area for around fifteen minutes. There is some evidence to suggest that this also has a secondary effect on the deeper blood vessels, greatly improving circulation.

### Physiotherapeutic Machines

There are a wide range of machines available to treat various ailments, most originating from human therapy and modified to suit equines. Their use is not yet commonplace and there are few practitioners compared to equine dentists or farriers.

Though some machines are available to unqualified therapists, it is strongly recommended they are only used by an expert following veterinary advice.

### Magnetic Field Therapy

This treatment is mainly used to assist in the healing process of bones, and works by passing a pulsed electro-magnetic field over the affected area. The pulses increase blood flow and circulation significantly, so the oxygen intake to the bone tissue increases and this promotes healing.

There are several machines available designed for animal use. There are mains operated units with magnets that can be positioned

There are several gels and sachets available that contain non-toxic gels which, following refrigeration, are bandaged to the horse's leg. They stay cold for three to five hours and are re-usable and very effective. Also widely available are boots and bandages impregnated with gel, that following refrigeration are applied directly to the leg and stay cool for around three hours. The boots are especially useful as they are quick to apply and stay in place well.

Commercially produced bonner bandages provide an instant cooling effect and provide support to a weak area. They contain ice crystals that melt against the horse's leg but their drawback is that they only stay cold for about fifteen minutes after refrigerating.

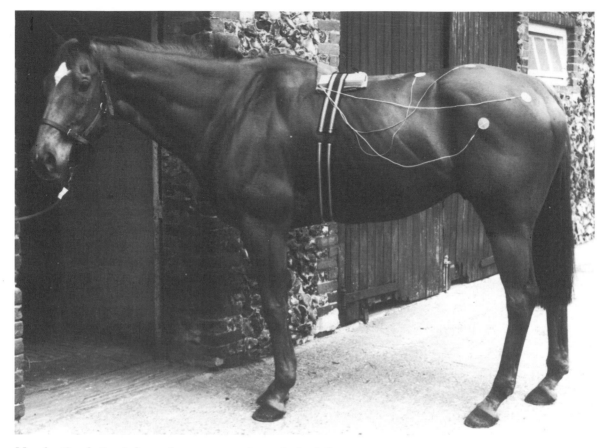

*Muscle stimulation is becoming a commonly used physiotherapy treatment.*

anywhere on the body, similar portable units powered by rechargeable batteries, and shoes and boots with a static magnetic field. The boots contain coated magnetic foil, which is also available in a pad or within rugs. Mains units are used for at least thirty minutes at a time, no more than once a day, whereas battery-powered machines can be used for a few hours a day, and static magnetic foil products continuously. The manufacturers will provide specific instructions with regard to treatment times. However, owing to a lack of clinical research, magnetic field therapy has not been widely used for injuries other than bone, though it has been applied to stimulate circulation in the treatment of strains, bruises and soft tissue damage.

### Direct Cell Stimulation

There are currently two machines available that stimulate the cell membranes within the body. They work by passing an electrical current to the ions (biological electric charges) at the centre of the cell, stimulating the production of new cells and tissue regeneration. These machines are battery charged and portable, and are strapped to the horse's body where the electrodes are attached to the desired area. One model can also stimulate the muscles so they alternately contract and relax, and is useful following muscle deterioration after either injury or strains. Direct cell stimulation has been successfully used to treat damaged tendons, joints, muscles, and also swellings.

## Muscle Stimulation

Faradic muscle stimulation machines have been used to treat humans for years, though only in recent times have they been used on animals. As such, some of the machines are not specifically designed with horses in mind. They work by sending a current to a muscle via electrodes, allowing it to contract around twenty times (this will differ according to treatment) before letting the muscle relax. Some machines are small and portable and can be strapped to the horse with a roller, so once the settings have been adjusted he can be treated with minimum fuss and intervention from the handler.

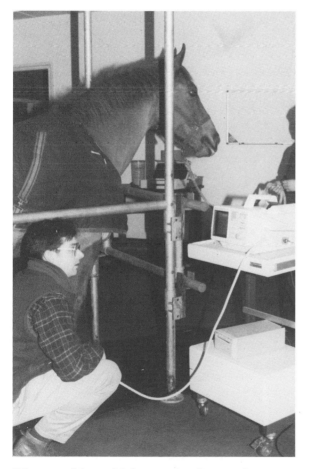

*Ultrasound is useful for treating damaged tendons.*

The stimulation treatment improves circulation and can assist in the rebuilding of muscles, and to a certain extent prevent further damage. The scar tissue surrounding previously damaged muscles may be reduced. As a result of its success in the field of human treatment, muscle stimulation therapy is more commonplace than some other physiotherapy treatments.

## Laser Therapy

Laser treatment involves high-frequency light vibration, and is used in the veterinary field in two ways. High or hot lasers are used surgically, to thicken, cut or destroy tissue, and low to medium cold lasers are used therapeutically to accelerate tissue healing. There are two types of cold laser machines used in equine therapy, the infra red and helium neon. Both accelerate collagen formation within the tissues to speed up the healing process.

It is suggested that laser therapy can be useful in the treatment of joint, bone, tendon muscle and ligament injuries, and also wounds. It can be used daily for seven to ten days, and positive results are usually apparent within a week.

## Ultrasound Therapy

Ultrasound is used for scanning, measurement, diagnosis and treatment and it is similar to magnetic field and laser therapy in that it effects the cells of the body. Ultrasound works by sending high frequency vibrating sound waves to the affected area, reducing muscle spasm and inflammation, and increasing the elasticity of scar tissue. Following cell activity it is suggested the previously damaged soft tissues are stronger, with more elasticity. Ultrasound can also be used on bone, minimizing cartilage production and speeding up the repair process.

## Additional Therapies

### Cell Therapy

Cell therapy consists of injected implants taken from healthy tissue, sometimes from an unborn foetus. The implant is injected in to the muscle or surrounding skin, and can reconstruct cells that have been damaged through injury or disease. The process has its risks, but these mainly concern horses with metabolic disorders or weak organs. The rehabilitation period must be carefully monitored, because if the horse is too active, his metabolism may use up the new cells for energy. Cell therapy is expensive and currently not widely used, though mainly carried out by naturopathic practitioners.

*Swimming Pool Therapy*

This is becoming increasingly popular as a conditioning and rehabilitation therapy for those with access to equine pools. It helps to develop muscle tone and promote circulation, as well as being enjoyable for most horses. As the weight is taken from the limbs, it is useful in the treatment of horses with leg disorders, as it allows their condition to improve without excess strain on the legs. As it is very tiring, the swimming time should increase gradually so the horse is not stressed. A heart monitor

*Swimming pool therapy is popular for both conditioning and rehabilitation.*

*Swimming pool therapy improves condition while imposing minimal external strain.*

should be used during and after swimming to ensure the heart rate is not too high, and that it returns to an acceptable level.

### Treadmill Therapy
The purpose of treadmill therapy is to exercise, monitor and make the horse fit with minimum foot and limb concussion. The angle of the treadmill can also be altered to enable the horse to work uphill, the muscles being worked unhindered by rider intervention.

### Back Manipulation
The subject of manipulation, usually carried out along the back, is a contentious one; even amongst veterinary surgeons and back

specialists' opinions. It would appear it is the terminology that causes this problem, as many manipulators claim a horse's back moves out. In fact, the vertebrae cannot be disturbed, and from withers to pelvis there is rarely any movement. A feasible explanation for the effects of manipulation is that practitioners work on the ligaments and muscles surrounding the bone surfaces, which can be and are often disturbed, unbalancing larger muscles and causing pain. By creating muscle contraction and relaxation, they cause the supporting muscles to re-balance themselves. However, if the original cause of the imbalance is still present (for example an old injury or incompetent rider) the problem may continue to recur.

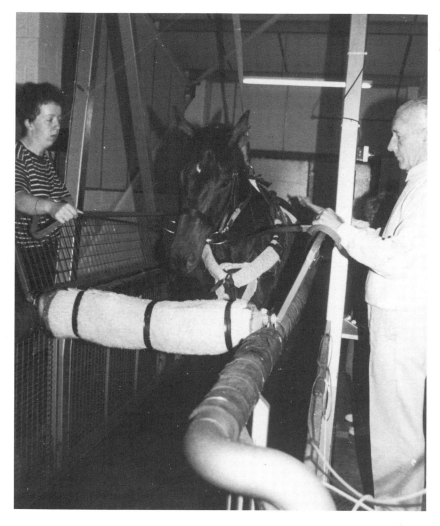

*Treadmill therapy can simulate various terrains and conditions.*

### Acupuncture

Acupuncture is an ancient Far Eastern method of treatment, which works on the concept of harnessing and balancing the natural energy force present in all living things by stimulating the various acupuncture points. For the treatment of horses, hypodermic needles or soft laser probes are used. Laser acupuncture probes can measure skin resistance and therefore accurately determine the siting of an acupuncture point. Equine acupuncture has been successfully used in the treatment of various disorders and relief of pain by strengthening the flow of the energy force.

### Shiatsu

This is a Japanese therapy that works on the same principles as acupuncture, utilizing the natural energy force. The therapist works on the acupuncture points, but rather than using needles, transfers his own energy to the horse via his hands, working as an energy channel. Though widely used on humans, particularly in Far Eastern cultures, *shiatsu* is not commonly used on equines and there are few practising therapists.

### Homoeopathy

Homoeopathic treatment has grown in popularity in recent years. It works on the principle

*Back manipulation should only be carried out by a reputable practitioner.*

of treating an ailment with a small dose of a substance that in larger doses would cause symptoms similar to the original illness. Though considered very 'alternative' to some, it is basically a method of treating like with like, working on the sensible premise of treating the whole animal and finding the root cause.

Homoeopathic remedies are most effective when absorbed through the mucous membranes of the mouth, usually in crushed or powdered form. There are many remedies available, too numerous to list here. However, some of the more well-known substances include: *arnica* to treat physical trauma (such as bruises and wounds), *phosphorus* for liver dysfunction, *opium* for limb concussion and

mental problems, and *belladonna* for heat-stroke. The use of homoeopathic remedies must only be carried out by a qualified homoeopathic practitioner, as many of the substances are poisonous if misused.

*Herbal Treatments*
Herbs have been used for years to maintain health and treat certain disorders, and are successfully used in the healing process of both humans and animals. The following herbs are a small cross-section of the wide range in popular use for the treatment of horses:
**Garlic** This is a widely used herb, given to horses for its healing properties. It is a very rich source of essential oils, vitamins and minerals,

useful for respiratory disorders, allergies, coughs and colds. It is also reported to cleanse the blood, and is used by some people to alleviate sweet itch and repel flies. It can be fed as crushed cloves or in liquid or powder form.

**Comfrey** A highly nutritious herb, used for healing and conditioning, and reportedly useful for the healing of wounds, strains and internal tissue formation. It can be used externally as a poultice, or given internally with the feed, either as cut leaves or within a supplement. Comfrey has also been reported to help arthritis and rheumatism.

**Clover** A nutritious plant, high in calcium and useful for alleviating skin conditions and adding condition. It is usually fed as a fresh or dried plant.

**Witch hazel** and **arnica** These are widely acclaimed for their antiseptic properties. They are used externally in distilled form for the treatment of sores, bruises, strains and swellings. Witch hazel is also an excellent anti-inflammatory.

---

ECONOMIZE

- An economical form of cold therapy is witch-hazel bandages. Soak gamgee or cotton wool in diluted distilled witch-hazel before bandaging the leg with it. The gamgee can be frozen in the shape of the leg for ice therapy.
- Human sunscreen is just as effective on horses as that supplied by the vet, although sweet smelling lotions may induce licking!
- Comfrey is a useful herb to grow in the garden. It can be fed freshly cut to horses, or used as a poultice as a cheap, effective herbal remedy.

---

# MAINTAINING A HEALTHY HORSE

## Hygiene

It is important to maintain a healthy environment at all times so disease is kept to a minimum. Tidying up and cleaning equipment need not take up too much time, and should be done on a daily basis to form part of the stable routine.

The following are basic hygiene guidelines:
- The grooming kit should be cleaned regularly so the brushes do their job, and are not putting dirt and germs back on to the horse. Each horse should have separate brushes, as disease will spread quickly if they are shared.
- All water buckets and feeding receptacles should be scrubbed daily, and field water containers cleaned out regularly. It is surprising how quickly scum can develop in a water tank, comprising sediment, leaves and dirt. As water is such an important part of the horse's body, it makes sense to keep the water supply clean and fresh.
- The stable should always be cleaned thoroughly, and the floor left to dry as often as possible. The dust content of the bedding should be kept to a minimum, as this can induce respiratory disorders. Good ventilation will also help to keep the air fresh and clean.
- All tack and equipment should be cleaned regularly. If there is not time to clean the tack daily, it helps to wipe it over after riding, cleaning it thoroughly every week. Rugs should be cleaned properly annually, but in the mean time brushed or vacuumed monthly to keep dirt at bay.
- The yard should be swept daily, and feed and storage rooms should be cleared at least every few days. This will not only keep dust and dirt to a minimum, but discourage vermin which carry all kinds of germs and spread disease very easily.
- The horse's field should be cleared of droppings regularly, particularly after the horse has been wormed. It is only when this task is left for days or weeks that it becomes time-consuming. The field shelter should ideally be mucked out at the same time, and if a layer of bed is put down it should be changed and renewed. With many horse owners having other responsibilities, it can be difficult to find the time for extra tasks. However, if they are done daily or weekly as part of the normal routine, they take up little time and make for a much healthier environment for both horse and owner.

## Parasitic Control

Having previously discussed worms and worming, it is also necessary to be aware of other parasites, in particular lice. They live off the horse's skin, biting and sucking blood and irritating the horse greatly. To a certain extent they can be avoided, as their life is made much easier by dirty horses, grooming brushes and tack. Lice eggs are easily transferred from horse to equipment and back again, the symptoms and itching appearing worse in the cold weather.

The lice only actually survive for a week off the horse, though their life cycle lasts around a month. Regular grooming and cleaning may help to keep the problem at a bearable level for the horse, though research suggests that the lice are present in most horses for more of the time than we realize. Treatment used to be with louse powder, though many chemically based brands contained a prohibited ingredient which has now been taken off the market. Herbal-based treatments may be effective in discouraging the lice in the same way as fly repellent, but infestation is controlled more effectively with insecticides. Veterinary surgeons can supply washes and treatments containing the relevant drugs, though they must be re-applied weekly. Rugs should also be treated, otherwise the lice will simply crawl back on the horse.

## Keeping Poisonous Plants at Bay

There are large numbers of poisonous plants growing in fields, gardens and hedgerows, in fact there are over fifty varieties in Great Britain. Fortunately, cases of plant poisoning are rare in horses, probably as a result of owners' vigilance in keeping the plants at bay. Also, horses find the taste of most poisonous plants unpleasant, using their highly developed senses of smell and taste to single them out from the tasty grass. Sadly there are some cases every year which are often fatal.

*Ragwort* is the most frequent cause of poisoning in horses, causing irreversible liver damage over a period of time. Although no one ragwort plant can kill a horse, when eaten over a period of weeks the toxins build up, so by the time owners notice the symptoms it may be too late. The plant is instantly recognizable by its pretty yellow flowers, and is commonly found in fields and gardens. It can be found in its equally poisonous dried state in hay as the crop is cut before the ragwort flowers appear. Unless owners are vigilant and check their hay before feeding, the plant may be accidentally eaten.

A horse suffering from ragwort poisoning may go off his food, have discoloured mucous membranes and be constipated. If the poisoning is diagnosed early enough and the source removed, veterinary treatment for the liver may save the horse. However there is no specific treatment, and the condition may well be fatal. Other potentially lethal plants include buttercups, hemlock, ivies, deadly nightshade, bryony, mare's-tail and wild arum. There are several trees and shrubs that must also never be eaten; yew is the most poisonous, and indeed is the most dangerous plant or tree a horse can eat. There are rarely any symptoms, and sudden death can occur within five minutes. Though yew trees are unlikely to grow in fields, they may be found in gardens or at church boundaries, and encountered on hacks. Other poisonous trees and shrubs include rhododendron, laburnum, bracken and privet. Acorns, oak tree leaves and conkers can also be deadly if eaten in sufficient quantities.

When removing poisonous plants or shrubs from the horse's field, they should be dug up from the roots and burned at a safe distance. There must be no opportunity for the horse to reach dangerous trees or shrubs over the fence. It is also important not to let the horse snatch a mouthful of foliage from a hedgerow when riding out, as this is where many of the poisonous shrubs grow untamed.

# 7 Bitting and Saddlery

The selection of tack available to the horse owner is extensive and even bewildering, with each manufacturer producing several variations on a certain product. Having previously discussed stable and field clothing, this chapter looks at the basic saddlery used by riders and horse owners, and its care and fitting. For an in-depth knowledge of the full range of equipment available, refer to an up-to-date manual or catalogue.

## THE BRIDLE

When moving without a rider, the horse has plenty of natural impulsion from the hindquarters, his head and neck steering the body in the desired direction. When the horse is backed and broken to saddle, the rider provides the desired impulsion with the legs and controls speed and direction with the bridle.

Bridles are traditionally made of leather, though some are available in webbing material. Leather is recommended because it is strong and durable, though the webbing is cheaper and easier to maintain. The bridle is made up of the following:

**The headpiece** This distributes the weight of the bridle and supports the bit. It lies directly behind the ears over the poll, and the throatlash and cheekpieces attach to the headpiece on either side.

**The cheekpieces** These hold the bit in the horse's mouth, taking pressure from the bit where it is applied at the poll. They should be of a sufficient length to allow several holes above and below the buckles for alteration and different sizes of bit ring.

**The throatlash** This prevents the bridle being pulled off over the ears in the case of an accident. It attaches to the headpiece at either side, and when secured correctly should allow a hand's breadth between the jowl and the throatlash, allowing the horse to breathe and flex the head with no restriction.

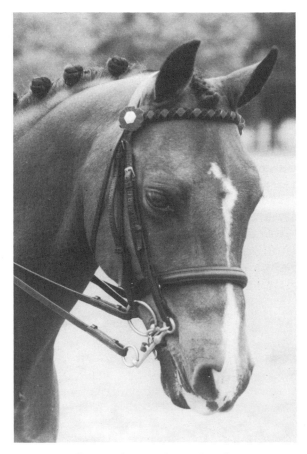

*Double bridles are frequently used in dressage and showing classes.*

**The browband** This prevents the bridle from slipping backwards. It attaches to the headpiece at either side of the head, sitting directly below the horse's ears across the forehead. At the correct length two finger's breadth should be allowed beneath the browband, so that it does not pinch the horse's ears or allow the headpiece to slip.

There are several styles of noseband available, all of which are suspended via a sliphead fitted beneath the headpiece; the *cavesson* is the most commonly used, positioned approximately four fingers' width above the nostrils; a *drop noseband* exerts pressure to the nose and encourages the horse to lower the head, resting at a lower point on the nose just above the end of the nasal bone. If it rests below the bone, it will restrict breathing and may pinch the skin. The back section fastens at the chin groove so the noseband is secured beneath the bit; the *flash noseband* is a combination of a cavesson and a drop, though the pressure point is higher up the nose – the lower strap passes around the muzzle below the bit, and prevents the horse crossing the jaw; *the grakle* consists of two loops of leather, fitted in a figure of eight design. It is similar to the flash, but has adjustable pressure points due to the moveable central piece through which the loops are threaded.

The last part of the bridle is the reins, the rider's means of communication regarding speed and direction. The reins attach to the bit rings and are available in various styles and thicknesses.

# BITS AND BITTING

There are seven points of bridle control on the horse's head: the tongue, lips, bars and roof of the mouth, and also the nose, poll and curb groove. According to the bit and bridle chosen, some or all of these points will be affected by the action of the equipment in conjunction with the rider's aids.

## A Summary of Bit Action

There are three main types of bit: snaffles, curbs, and Pelhams, though additional groups include gags and double bridles. Generally speaking, bits belonging to the snaffle family act on three of the points: the tongue, bars and lips, though the other points may also be affected with certain bits. The action may be increased when nosebands such as grakles, drops and flashes are used, as the nose and chin groove are also affected. *Curb-bits* act on the tongue, bars, lips, poll and curb groove, and may also affect the roof of the mouth if port mouthpieces are added. *The Pelham* works on the same points as the snaffle and the curb combined, and the *gag snaffle* on the tongue, bars, lips, cheeks and the poll. The double bridle has two mouthpieces and

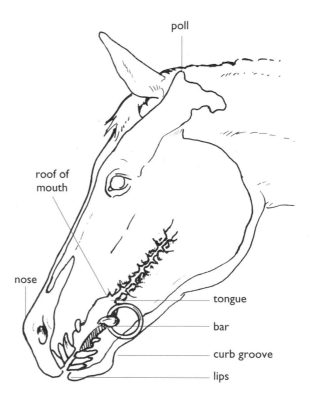

*Seven points of control.*

therefore double pressure on the tongue, bars, and lips, and single pressure on the roof of the mouth and chin groove.

It is plain to see that with so many combined actions, even the most gentle bit can cause severe pressure if put in the wrong hands. By changing the noseband, the affect can increase furthermore, so unsympathetic or careless riding may cause considerable pain. This is when the horse may try to evade the action or flee from pain, and get a chastizing jab in the mouth from his thoughtless rider. It is very important to understand the effects of the various bits, as a horse with a damaged mouth may never accept the contact properly again.

## Selecting a Bit

It is fair to say that a certain number of riders classify a bit according to a generalized opinion of its severity, with little thought given to their riding. For some riders it seems a cut and dried affair, assuming that gags and doubles are severe and all snaffles are kind. In reality, the lightness and experience of the rider makes all the difference. Even a snaffle that exerts minimum pressure becomes severe in ignorant hands. Therefore owners should assess their own riding when choosing a bit, as it is quite likely that the horse will go nicely in a milder bit if he is ridden with sympathetic hands.

There are three main materials used for bits: *stainless steel*, which suits most horses but is hard and unyielding; *vulcanized rubber* which is softer and more comfortable; and various synthetic materials that are even softer and useful for sensitive mouths. *Nickel* or other inferior metal bits are widely available second-hand but not advised for use, as the edges can get sharp with wear. Horses may favour one type of material over another, though their preference will be established only through practical trying-out sessions. There are also other considerations that may affect the horse's way of going, such as a sore

mouth, sharp teeth or physical problems such as back pain. These factors must all be eliminated before selecting a different bit.

## Fitting a Bit

It is important that whatever style the horse's bit is, it must fit correctly and comfortably. Thus the size of the horse's mouth must be taken into consideration, as all horses are built slightly differently.

Mullen or straight-barred bits may sit quite close to the sides of the horse's lips, as once fitted there is little movement within the mouth. Jointed bits have more movement so can allow a little more room either side of the lips for mobility. They may also wrinkle the corners more due to their shape when correctly fitted.

*A bit that is too large may pull unevenly through one side of the mouth and cause discomfort.*

Therefore jointed bits may be of a slightly larger size, though no more than a quarter of an inch. As a general rule, the horse should have a few wrinkles at the corners of the lips when wearing the bit, but not look as though he is grinning. The bit itself is measured in inches, from the inside of the bit rings when it is laid flat.

## Snaffles

It is ultimately desirable for all horses to go well in the mildest possible bit, so the sensible place to start is with the snaffle family. There are seven basic types of snaffle mouthpiece, and ten basic cheek styles. So already, without even looking at the individual bits, it is clear there are many variations, as the mouth- and cheekpieces combined will all produce different actions.

## Mouthpieces

**Mullen mouthpieces** These are not jointed, and act on the tongue, lips and corners of the mouth. They are slightly curved and quite mild, especially if they have a thick mouthpiece made from rubber or vulcanite. Most horses are quite comfortable with them.

**Straight-bar mouthpieces** Similar to mullen mouths in their appearance and pressure points, but they have no curve so the pressure is slightly increased, particularly over the tongue.

**Single jointed mouthpieces** These have a slight nutcracker action on the tongue, putting pressure on the lips and bars to varying degrees, depending on the shape of the arms either side of the joint. The more curved the arms, the milder the action.

**Double-jointed mouthpieces** are joined in

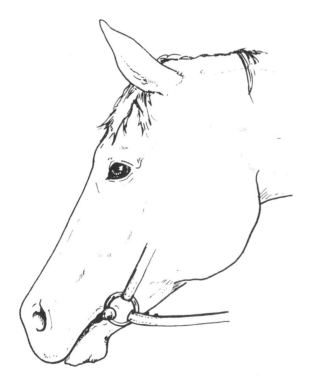

*A bit correctly fitted.*

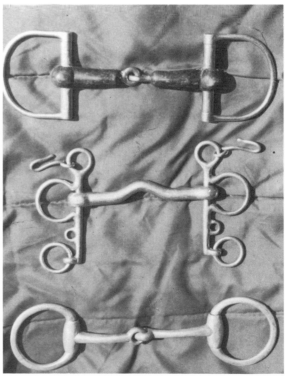

*The range of bit types, materials, mouthpieces and styles available is extensive and potentially bewildering (see also overleaf).*

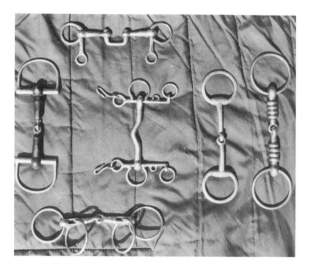
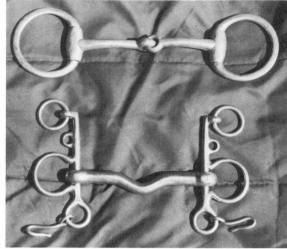

*More of the bewildering range of bit types.*

the centre by a smooth plate. This allows each arm more mobility but less space in the mouth for the tongue, so when the horse is not flexing his head properly, pressure is applied there. The nutcracker action is lost, so the main pressure points are the lips and bars.

**Rollered mouthpieces** Straight-barred, jointed or ported, these act upon the tongue, lips, corners, and in the case of ported versions, the roof of the mouth. Their main purpose is to allow the horse to play with the bit and salivate, and also prevent him from taking hold of it and evading.

**Ported mouthpieces** These allow more room for the tongue as they have a raised central section. This in turn allows more pressure on the roof and corners of the mouth, in addition to the lips.

**Spooned mouthpieces** These are not at all widely used, and incorporate a flat central plate so that the horse is unable to get his tongue over the bit. They are less comfortable than ported mouthpieces, but usually achieve the same end result.

*Bit-cheek Styles*

There are five styles of loose-ring bit-cheeks with mobile rings running through the mouthpiece: flat rings, loose rings, loose-ringed bridoons (for use with double bridles), and Fulmers. (These all feature small rings allowing plenty of movement and a light contact, and guidance in the case of Fulmers.) Lastly, wire rings, which are much larger and provide a guiding action for youngsters and are commonly used for racehorses.

Two of the other cheek styles are fixed to the mouthpiece; the *eggbut*, which has little movement but will not pinch the lips; and the *D-ring* for cheek guidance and to prevent the bit being pulled through the mouth. The remaining three cheek styles are not fixed but due to their additional cheekpieces they have minimal movement. They are the *full cheek*, which has little movement but provides guidance, the *hanging cheek*, which rests on the tongue and hangs in the mouth, and the *spoon cheek*, which is often used in harness racing, preventing the bit from being pulled through the mouth.

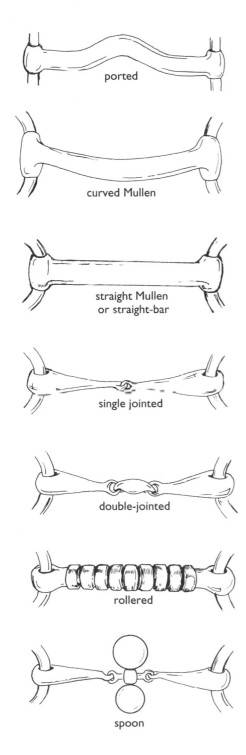

*Types of mouthpiece.*

Bit-cheeks have a lesser effect on the pressure points than the mouthpieces, though they may affect the lips, bars and cheeks. The mouthpiece is usually the most important consideration. The bit cheeks add a certain action for specific problems, such as a leaning contact, the need for guidance when steering, or to prevent the bit's being pulled to one side of the mouth.

## Types of Snaffle

As there are so many different snaffles available, it is not feasible to list them all here, so the most commonly used styles are given.

### Jointed Eggbut
This is one of the most popular snaffles, used for well-mannered horses and youngsters as it is mild and comfortable. It puts pressure on the tongue, bars and lips and is useful when asking sideways flexion of the horse, particularly as the arms either side of the join move independently of one another.

### Mullen Mouth Loose Ring
These put pressure on the tongue, bars and lips, and are also useful for young horses. Providing the horse is well-mannered they are useful for schooling, as the rein contact will be light due to the moveable mouthpiece.

### German Hollow-mouth
This is a single-jointed bit, very lightweight and thick, and therefore comfortable for the horse. The affected pressure points are the tongue, bars and lips, and the bit-cheeks may be eggbut or loose ring.

### D-ring/Racing Snaffle
This bit has a single join, putting pressure on the bars, lips, and tongue. The arms are fairly thin so the bit can be quite severe. The D-rings help to prevent the bit being pulled through the mouth, and also help to keep it still and square.

## Fulmer

These long-cheeked bits work on the lips, bars, tongue and cheeks, providing a guiding action which is useful on young horses. They are single or double-jointed and may be fixed at the cheekpieces putting extra pressure on the bars, the loose rings allowing plenty of movement.

## French Link

This double-jointed bit has a flat plate link, which is comfortable for most horses and provides mobility within the mouth. Though the single-joint nutcracker action is lost, horses with larger tongues may find the French link uncomfortable. It is available with eggbut, loose ring or Fulmer cheeks, and puts pressure on the lips and bars and, to a certain extent, the tongue.

## Dr Bristol

At first glance this double-jointed bit is similar to the French link, though the plate link is angled and therefore more severe. However, when used upside-down the action is greatly reduced. It has the same pressure points as the French link, but also adds pressure to one or both sides of the tongue. It is available with eggbut, loose ring, Fulmer or D-ring cheeks.

## Dick Christian

This double-jointed bit is very similar in action and appearance to the French link above, although instead of a plate there is a small ring at the centre, which reduces tongue pressure. It is very useful for horses with sensitive mouths.

## Fillis

This is a ported, hanging cheek snaffle that is suspended within the mouth and is quite comfortable for the horse. It puts pressure on the corners of the lips, and also the poll, though the poll action is only apparent when the horse raises his head sufficiently.

## Filet Baucher

This bit has evolved from the Fillis, and is a single or double-jointed eggbut with hanging cheeks. As there is no port, it is more severe than the Fillis and puts additional pressure on the tongue, though the lips and poll are affected in the same way.

## Cherry Roller

This is a single-jointed snaffle with rollers set around the arms. It is designed so the horse mouths and salivates, and cannot get hold of the bit. It puts pressure on the tongue, bars and lips, and is available with eggbut, loose ring, D-ring or Fulmer cheeks.

## Magenis

This is a single-jointed bit with horizontal rollers set within square arms. It encourages the horse to mouth the bit and it prevents him from crossing his jaw, putting pressure on the tongue, bars and lips, commonly loose-ringed.

## Wilson

This is a single-jointed, four-ringed bit, the cheek pieces attaching to inner mobile rings. It puts normal pressure on the tongue and lips, and extra pressure on the bars and cheeks. The skin around the cheeks and the lips can easily be pinched, so this is a severe bit to use and care should be taken.

## Scorrier

This is similar to the Wilson in action and pressure points, though the inner rings are fixed so that the lip pinching action is lessened. However, it still exerts pressure to the cheeks and jaw, and also on the tongue as one side of the mouthpiece is twisted. Both Scorriers and Wilsons should be used only in knowledgeable hands.

## Belgian Three-ring

This snaffle bit can also be classified as a curb or gag, depending on which of the three rings the reins are attached to. It has a single joint,

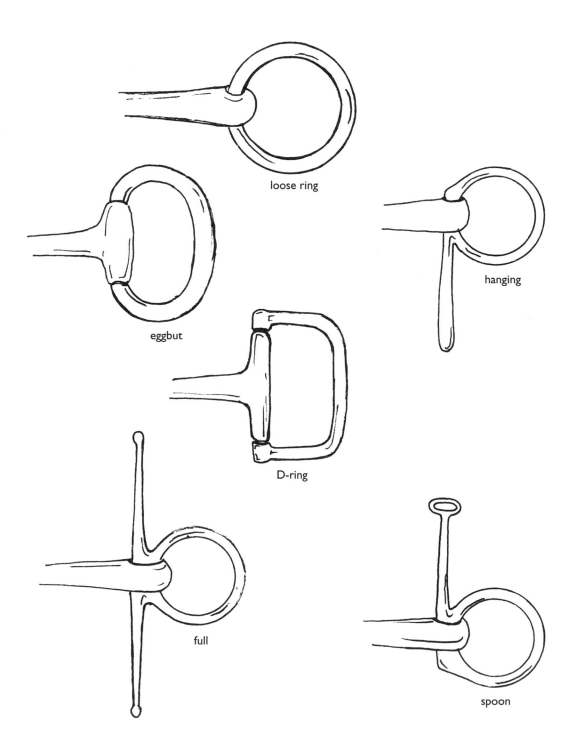

loose ring

eggbut

hanging

D-ring

full

spoon

*Bit cheek styles.*

117

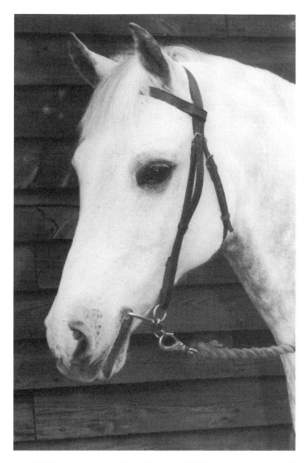

*A chiffney is a training bit, useful for restraint and for disobedient youngsters.*

### KK Schooling and Correction Bits

These are German bits, available in three styles for various stages in the horse's training. The first is a training bit, similar to a loose-ring French link in pressure points and action, though the link is rounder with a greater weight-bearing surface. The second is a schooling bit, with eggbut cheeks, a wide port and angled arms. It eliminates pinching and puts minimal pressure on the bars and lips. The last KK bit is a correction bit, with a wide port, angled arms and loose rings which add pressure to the bars and reduces leaning. Other manufacturers are currently developing their own alternatives to these bits.

## Types of Curb

Curb-bits come in three styles of mouthpiece: *plain mullen mouths*, which act on the tongue and the bars; *arched or port mouths*, which allow varying amounts of tongue space and bar pressure; and the *Cambridge mouth*, with low port and extra bar pressure. Curbs are used within the double bridle in conjunction with bridoons, which are scaled down snaffles with small rings to give a close contact with the rider. It is usual to use an eggbut bridoon with a fixed curb, and a loose ring in conjunction with a sliding-cheek curb.

Within knowledgeable hands, curb-bits can be used on their own, inducing extra pressure on the chin groove and poll, and to a certain extent the roof of the mouth. They are used in conjunction with curb-chains (which may be leather or rubber covered) that rest within the curb groove, attached at either side of the bit and secured with a lip strap.

In addition to those mentioned below, there are other types of curb including Western and showing bits, but they are quite severe and not in common use nowadays.

### Tom Thumb

This is the mildest curb bit, with a wide mouthpiece, short cheeks and minimal action when used in the right hands.

and when used on the large top ring has the same effect as a loose ring snaffle. In theory, the further down the reins are positioned, the more severe the action, pressure increasing on the bars, lips and most noticeably the poll.

### Conrad Universal

This is similar to the Belgian three-ring, featuring a single joint and two rings to which the reins are attached. When the top ring is used it has the same action as a loose ring, though when the lower ring is used, a more severe curb action is induced with extra poll pressure. It can be used with two reins in a similar way to a Pelham.

## Sliding Cheek

This is a commonly used curb bit within the double bridle, with slightly longer cheeks than the Tom Thumb. It allows movement within the mouth, but provides control and comfort when the horse is relaxed. When the slide rises, the poll pressure increases, encouraging the horse to lower his head.

## Dressage Weymouth

This German bit is hollow with a Cambridge port and longer fixed cheeks. It is commonly used for three day eventing, and its broad mouthpiece makes it comfortable.

## Banbury Curb

The mouthpiece of this bit fits into a slot, allowing it to slide up and down and revolve. This makes each rein that little bit more independent, and allows the horse to mouth freely. Instead of a port the centre is hourglass shaped, thus adding pressure to the tongue.

## Globe Cheek

These bits are not used within double bridles as the cheeks are so short, and the large rings would look unsightly and could interfere with the bridoon. They usually have a ported mouthpiece, with pressure applied to the bars but little on the poll.

## Types of Pelham

Pelham bits are usually used by riders who find a snaffle insufficient, but dislike using two bits. Essentially the Pelham is a hybrid, combining curb and snaffle action. However, they are only truly effective on certain horses with knowledgeable riders, as some animals just shorten their top line rather than flexing properly. The Pelham is designed to encourage a light, forward-going action with correct flexion, and this only occurs when two reins are used. The use of roundings to which one rein is attached defeats the object somewhat, and the Pelham simply becomes a severe snaffle with poll action. Pelhams are available in several materials, but seem most popular in rubber or vulcanite, as the mouthpiece is thick and more comfortable than metal.

## Mullen Mouth / Half Moon

This is a common type of Pelham, designed to relieve tongue pressure. The cheeks come in varying lengths and may have eggbut or turning cheek sides. The latter turn from left to right but not up and down, and allow movement and a lighter contact.

## Rugby Pelham

This bit is the most similar in both appearance and action to the double bridle, as the loose bridoon link is attached to the Pelham cheek. It has a well defined action on the curb groove and poll, and is commonly used in the show ring.

## Scamperdale

This is a fixed-cheek, straight-bar Pelham which is angled at the sides, reducing bar pressure and rubbing of the mouth and cheeks. The shape of the bit means that the curb-chain rarely works in the correct place, so it may be used without one.

## Arch Mouth Pelham

The mouthpiece of this bit has an upward curve, allowing plenty of room for the tongue and adding pressure to the bars of the mouth.

## SM Pelham

The mouthpiece of this bit is a wide plate bent into an arch which works as a swivel, providing a wide weight-bearing surface on the bars. The cheekpieces are angled away from the face so there is no friction on the cheeks.

## Hannovarian

This bit has long cheeks and a high port which is hinged, and there are cherry rollers at each side of the port. This is commonly used for polo ponies, as it is far more suited to sharp turns and stops, but it seems rather too severe to use when schooling.

*Hartwell*
This bit has a reasonably short sliding cheeks and a small port, putting pressure on the bars but allowing movement. In appearance it is similar to a Weymouth curb.

*Jointed Pelhams*
These are available in several materials and cheek lengths, adding the nutcracker action to the tongue.

*Kimblewick*
This is a combination of a snaffle and a normal Pelham, using one rein and a curb-chain. When the rider's hands are lowered a curb action is induced, and pressure on the poll increases. The most common Kimblewick has a Cambridge mouth, though other mouthpieces are available.

## Types of Gag

The gag is actually a form of snaffle, though quite severe in some cases due to the downward pressure on the poll. It is most effective when used as a temporary schooling aid for a few weeks, as permanent use may confuse the horse. Most snaffles ask for an element of elevation, but the pressure of the leverage produced by some gags may contradict this. Light hands are essential, as excess pressure may cause the horse to back off from the contact or rear. For some strong horses, gags may be the only long-term answer, but fortunately these cases are rare.

Though there are over five types of gag available most are not widely used and are reserved for the serious trainer. For this reason the two gags most commonly used by the one-horse owner (as opposed to competition yards and businesses), are listed.

*Gag Snaffle*
The cheekpieces of this bit pass through holes in the top and bottom of the bit cheeks, putting pressure on the corners of the lips and the poll and providing poll leverage. The gag gives a lot of control as most horses respect it, and it should be used in conjunction with another rein attached to the bit ring. This way the gag rein need only come into play when necessary, so it can be used to make a point and shock the horse, rather than being continually used and abused.

*American Gag*
This bit has a curb rein attached to the rings at the end of the bit cheeks, which are long and angled, and produce severe poll pressure. As with all gags, it is most useful as a temporary measure, and when used with an additional rein at the side of the central bit ring is less severe.

# SADDLES

There are many makes and different styles of saddles available, giving riders a wide range of choice. It is vital the saddle fits well, is in a safe, good condition and provides comfort for both the horse and its rider. A suitable saddle places the rider in the centre of gravity for whatever discipline it is designed for, so certain saddles are designed with certain activities in mind, such as show jumping, dressage or showing.

## Saddle Design

*The Tree*
The tree is essentially the skeleton that supports the rest of the saddle, traditionally made from beechwood but often incorporating glass-fibre or synthetic materials such as polymer. There are three types of tree: the *traditional rigid* version, which is rarely favoured as it does not 'give' with the horse's movement; the *spring tree*, which is the most popular, allowing more resilience in the seat; and the *adjustable tree*, with a shape can be slightly altered to allow for the horse changing shape. Trees are available in three width fittings: narrow, standard and wide.

*A correctly fitting saddle should be comfortable for both horse and rider.*

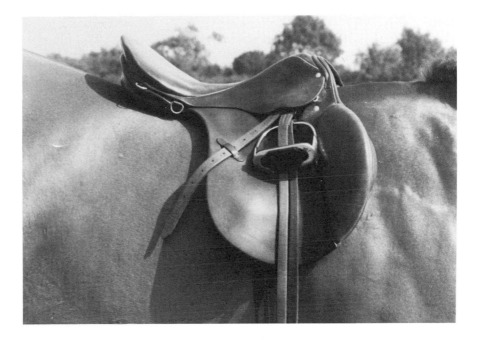

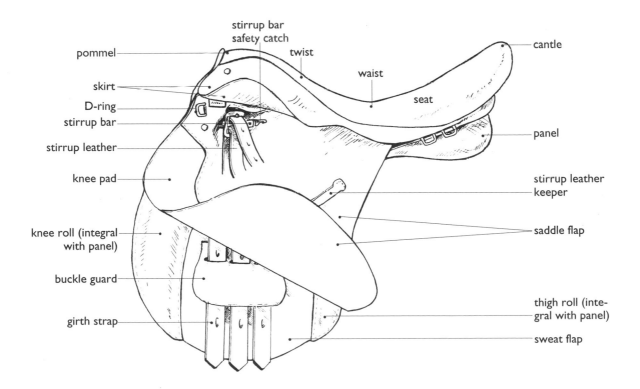

*Points of an English Saddle.*

121

## Length

The length of the saddle is measured in inches, allowing for the various size of horse and length of back. The short-backed horse fitted with a long saddle will be forced to bear the weight of it on his loins, while the long-backed horse fitted with a long saddle is likely to become sore as the saddle's weight will be concentrated on one small area of his back. Since no two horses of the same height are of the same shape, each horse should be fitted individually. Saddles are available in various shapes to suit the individual.

## Stuffing

The saddle is stuffed to relieve pressure on the horse's back and provide comfort. Saddles mould to the shape of the horse, so his level of fitness and schooling may influence the fit. New saddles will need re-stuffing periodically as the stuffing will 'bed down' to the shape of the horse. Saddles should not be shared for this purpose, as they will not fit any horse properly and may cause soreness.

## Materials

Traditionally saddles have always been made from leather. Though there is a wide variety of quality available, some inferior leather is best avoided. Quality leather saddles are durable and attractive if well looked after, and mould well to the rider's shape. Synthetic saddles have become popular in recent years, and are much cheaper than leather. Though some older synthetic saddles were not very attractive, most newer versions are pleasing to the

*Both synthetic and leather saddles have their advantages and disadvantages.*

eye, are easy to clean and very lightweight. The choice of material comes down to personal preference, as both types have their dedicated followers. In my own opinion, the leather saddle may have the edge appearance wise, but synthetic versions are much more economical in terms of time and money.

## Fitting

It is advisable for all saddles to be fitted by a saddler or experienced person, whether they be new or second hand. Some retailers offer a fitting service, which may be free if they sell you a saddle. However it is important to know the basics of saddle fitting, especially as the horse may change shape over a period of time:

- The saddle should be fitted without a numnah or cloth.
- It should not be in contact with the withers (a gap of three fingers is suggested between withers and pommel of the saddle).
- The gullet on the underside of the saddle should clear the spine completely, and daylight should be seen when looking from the cantle to the pommel. The panels either side of the gullet should lie comfortably along the horse's back, with no point pinching or raised in any way. A gap of four fingers is suggested between the spine and underside of the cantle.
- The side panels should not hinder movement but lie against the shoulders, at no point pinching or causing pressure.
- With a rider on board, the gullet and pommel

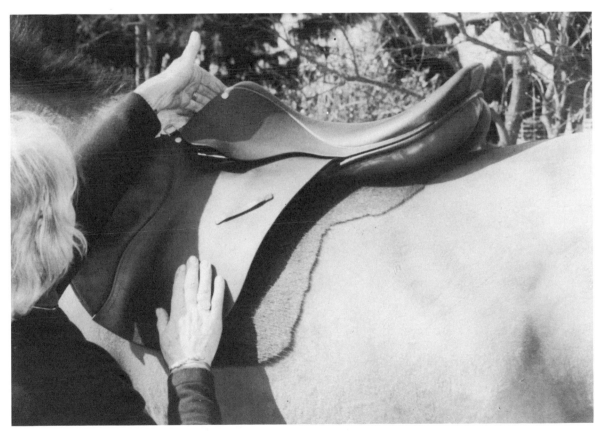

*It is important to have the saddle correctly and safely fitted by a professional.*

should still clear the spine and withers respectively, and the cantle should not lift up. The rider should be in the centre of balance.

- The saddle must look right, that is not too large or small. When correctly positioned the cantle should be slightly higher than the pommel, and should fit snugly to the horse's shape, not moving around which will cause friction and soreness.

## Styles of Saddle

### General Purpose (GP)
As the name implies, this saddle is literally designed for general-purpose riding, so the average rider who does a little of everything, from hacking to jumping, will find it suitable. It is essentially a cross between the jumping and dressage saddle, offering a cushioned seat, slight knee rolls and a good contact between the rider's seat and the horse's back. The serious competitor may choose to purchase separate saddles for different disciplines, but for the rider who competes at local level, the GP will be perfectly adequate.

### Jumping
The jumping saddle, as we know it, was introduced at the turn of the twentieth century, to cope with the new forward seat introduced by a Russian Cavalry School rider. The forward seat took the rider's weight forward, allowing the hindquarters to move freely and with more impulsion. Thus, the modern jumping saddle has a rounded, forward cut panel and a more pronounced knee roll, allowing for balance and comfort with the rider's weight still in the centre of gravity.

### Dressage
The dressage saddle has been designed to allow for the rider's classical upright position, incorporating straighter panels and a large weight distribution area, with the rider's centre of gravity moving further back. Most dressage saddles have small knee and thigh rolls to support the leg and encourage a deep seat

and long leg position. Some also have short Lonsdale girths that buckle beneath the leg flap, to enhance comfort and appearance.

### Other Styles
There are other styles of saddle designed for specific purposes, including eventing, showing, racing, hunting, endurance, and side-saddle. These all incorporate special features to enhance the rider's effectiveness for the particular discipline, or add to the horse's comfort, and are available in an equally wide range. One recent innovation is a saddle with interchangeable knee rolls, suitable for general riding, jumping or dressage. The competitor can purchase one saddle and comfortably compete in several disciplines without using different saddles.

## Accessories

### Girths
Girths are used to keep the saddle in place, and pass behind the elbows to rest in the sternum groove in front of the horse's belly. They must be fitted correctly to ensure safety, and also comfort of the horse. A loose girth is in danger of not holding the saddle in place, causing it to slip forwards or backwards, or worse still, sideways. It should be done up gradually so it does not pinch, and a hand should be run underneath the girth to smooth the skin of wrinkles. Gently pulling a foreleg forward will also reduce wrinkles, and is especially useful when using girths with elasticated sections, which may trap sections of skin. It is general practice to check and tighten the girth three times; firstly when the saddle is placed on the horse's back; just before the rider mounts; and lastly after the horse has walked around. He may have been blowing the belly out beforehand, but will have relaxed a little more at this point.

### Stirrup Leathers and Irons
Leathers pass through the eyes of the stirrup irons and attach at the bars outside the saddle

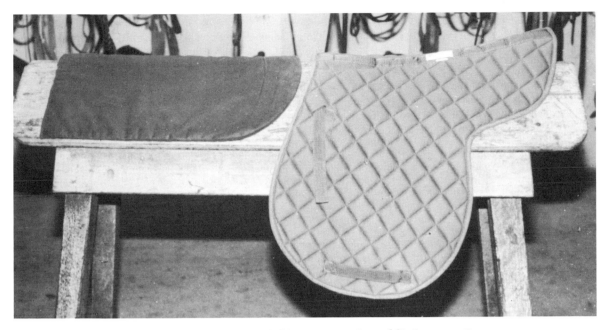

*There are various numnahs and gel pads available to protect the saddle from scurf and grease, and the horse's back from shock and concussion.*

flap. They are fully adjustable to cater for the rider's leg length, and must be in good, strong condition to prevent breakage. They are usually numbered from their base upwards so that riders can check they are of an equal length.

The irons give riders support and secure the position, and come in a variety of sizes to accommodate different feet. Obviously, it is imperative the irons are of a suitable size – too large and the foot could pass right through, too small and it could get wedged. Stirrup treads are used to provide a non-slip surface for the rider's feet, and are fitted within the hole of the stirrup iron.

### Numnahs and Pads
There are many forms of under-saddle protection available for horses at present, designed for a variety of purposes including to reduce pressure, to provide comfort, absorb moisture and keep the saddle clean. It is important that the numnah or pad is used for a specific purpose, as the fit of the saddle will be influenced,

especially if they are quite thick. They should not be used to compensate for ill-fitting tack, but can be beneficial for certain horses, particularly those in high performance work. Most equine manufacturers produce a range of styles, such as gel-filled pads that absorb shock and relieve pressure points, and numnahs that absorb moisture and therefore reduce friction and heat.

### Breastplates
These prevent the saddle from slipping backwards, and are often used in circumstances where the tack is under strain from fast movement or athleticism, such as racing or eventing. There are two styles in common use: the *hunting breastplate*, through which the girth passes, attaching to the rings at the top of the saddle; and the *racing breastgirth*, which attaches beneath the saddle flaps and rests over the neck. They should not be used to compensate for an ill-fitting saddle, but should ensure stability and comfort.

125

*Cruppers*

These are used to prevent the saddle from slipping forwards, and are fitted beneath the tail, attaching to the rear of the saddle. They are commonly used on ponies with ill-defined withers and fat bellies, or on driving horses to secure the harness.

# TRAINING AIDS

There are many training aids on the market which have been designed to assist riders with certain problems they might encounter. They are designed to assist, that is to be used in conjunction with correct schooling, and should not be considered a short cut to desirable results. They should be used by a knowledgeable rider, and only until their purpose has been served. It may be easy to rely on them and use them as an easy option for longer than is necessary.

## Martingales

Martingales are the most common schooling aids, used to great effect to lower the horse's head carriage and assist him in finding his own balance. If it is possible, they should be used as a temporary measure while the rider tries to sort the problem out, though many people use them on a long-term basis.

There are three basic styles: the *running martingale*, which attaches on to the girth at one end, and reins at the other by means of small rings. These are only restrictive when the horse's head is raised above the desired height, and are commonly used by trainers and riders; the *standing martingale*, which is more restrictive and attaches to the girth and the back of the noseband. These have the effect of holding the horse's head in, rather than suggesting a comfortable position, and should be used with discretion; and the *combined martingale*, which is literally a combination of the two, and quite severe if used in the wrong hands.

The *Irish martingale* is not a training aid, but a means of preventing the reins from passing over the horse's head in the event of a fall. It is simply a leather strap with two rings at either side, through which the reins pass.

## Balancing Reins and Gadgets

This heading covers the multitude of artificial aids used on equines, about which entire books are written. There are many types available to work on various problems, some in the form of reins, some in the form of pulleys and most somewhere in between. The term 'gadget' is rarely endorsed by the various manufactures, but in this case serves as a general term for the many aids available. They are undoubtedly useful in a multitude of cases, but a thorough knowledge of the action on the bit or carriage of the horse must precede use. It is recommended that a riding instructor or knowledgeable person supervises from the ground, so a full picture of their effectiveness is achieved.

# CARE OF THE TACK

It is important to keep all tack in good working order, which includes regular cleaning and maintenance. In theory, tack should be cleaned after each use, but this may be quite impractical. Providing the tack is wiped down after each use, it may be thoroughly cleaned on a weekly basis, taking it apart and checking for damage such as loose stitching or split leather.

## Care of Leather

When cleaning leather, the tack should first be stripped, which means that the bridles should be taken apart and the girths and leathers removed from saddles. The bit and stirrup irons can be placed in a bucket of warm water to soak while the leather itself is being cleaned.

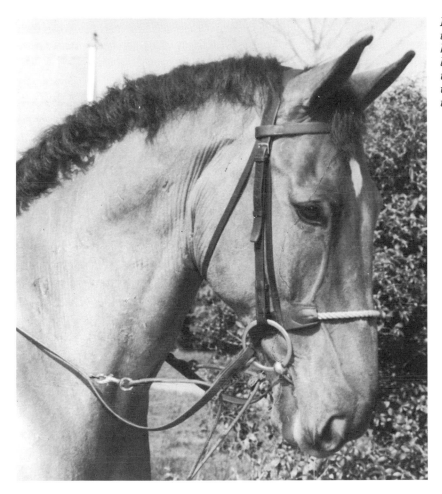

*Balancing reins and other training aids are useful for horse's with schooling problems, but they should be used only under the supervision of an experienced trainer or handler.*

Firstly, any excess mud or dirt should be removed with a cloth or soft brush. Then using a sponge, the tack should be cleaned with warm water. This involves wringing the sponge out so there is no excess moisture, then applying pressure to each part of the leather using a gentle rubbing action. This should be done until all the grease is removed, and in the case of dirty tack may take a few applications. Once each piece of tack has been washed, providing it is not wet, it may be soaped with saddle soap. This keeps it supple and gives a deep shine. The same sponge may be used, but it should be thoroughly wrung out as too much soap will create an undesirable lather. The same rubbing action is used, re-applying the soap every so often to ensure an even covering. When the tack has a sheen and feels supple, enough soap has been applied. Tack in poor condition, which is quite dry or stiff, may need several applications.

The bit and irons should be removed and dried, and the tack put back together again. Then a final polish with the sponge will remove any finger prints and make it look that little bit smarter. There are several additional treatments available for cleaning tack, such as oils and creams, and these are suited to tack in varying conditions and use. They are generally used as a complimentary treatment to saddle soap, though some may replace the soaping process and use different ingredients. The relevant manufacturers' instructions should always be followed.

## Care of Synthetics

As the exact type of synthetic materials will differ according to the manufacturer, it is suggested advice is sought if in any doubt regarding care. However, most synthetic saddles can simply be gently scrubbed with water and a little washing-up liquid, then rinsed with a hose. Their nap can be brushed up with a soft nail brush once they are dry, making them very easy to maintain. Webbing is washed in a similar way, but holds water for a long while. It may be preferable to brush it thoroughly then wash the surface with water without soaking.

*The care and cleaning of tack and equipment is important, and must be carried out regularly.*

---

### ECONOMIZE

- Try before you buy. When choosing a bit, find a saddlery that offers a 'bit library service'. An unsuitable bit may usually be returned within a few days saving unnecessary expense.
- Second-hand saddlery departments are useful places to find cheap bits. Any that are noticeably worn or damaged should be discarded, but there are bargains in good condition available.
- Synthetic saddlery is made to a high standard and can even look like leather. A new synthetic saddle can be bought for less money than an inferior second-hand leather one.

# 8 Travelling

Most horses at some stage in their life will travel in a horse box or trailer and some horses who compete at shows and events will make several journeys each week. A lot of the potential trauma can be removed from travelling with good preparation; with a little foresight, common sense and safety precautions, travelling the horse need not become an arduous task. Here are some points owners should remember:

## THE HORSE

- Most horses are initially a little nervous of loading and travelling. It is useful if owners have access to boxes or trailers, to get the horse used to them in advance, walking him up the ramp daily and allowing him to eat his feed inside. This way he associates loading with a pleasant experience.

*Most horses will have to travel in a horse-box or trailer at some time during their lives.*

- It will also be useful to take the horse on a few small journeys before travelling a long distance, so he gets used to the motion of the journey and learns to balance himself.
- Prior to loading, the horse should be groomed and prepared for the show (including plaiting), so if any problems are encountered and time is lost, there is be little work to be done on arrival.
- It is best to leave the horse's travel clothing until just before loading, as some seasoned travellers associate the clothes with excitement and may break out in sweat.
- The horse should be fed at least an hour before travelling, so the digestion process is not interfered with by excitement, stress or sweating.

## THE TRAILER OR HORSEBOX

- If hiring transport, a reputable firm should be chosen, as any breakdown could be disastrous with a horse on board.
- The hired vehicle should be scrupulously clean, as any germs or infection from previous horses could be passed on.
- The vehicle should be taken out for a practice run the day before the show, as if it has not been used for some time the battery may be flat.
- All vehicles should be checked to make sure the lights and indicators work and are wired up correctly.

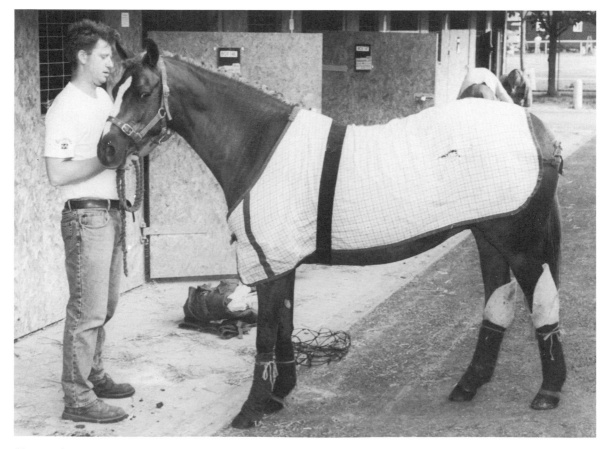

*Horses should be properly protected for travelling like the horse in this picture.*

*The horse in this picture is also wearing knee boots and a tail bandage, and the handler is also more sensibly dressed.*

- The petrol or diesel should be checked and filled in advance, so there is no need to make unnecessary stops with the horse on board – this could be stressful for the horse, who may think he has arrived at his destination.
- Safety checks should be made on the flooring and ramps to make sure they have not rotted or become unstable.
- Details of the vehicle's height and weight should be kept in the horsebox cab in case the journey entails driving under low bridges or over those with weight restrictions.
- Clean matting or bedding should be laid down in advance, and a loop of breakable twine attached to the tying-up ring.

## EQUIPMENT

It will be useful to make a list of all the necessary equipment, ticking the items off as they are loaded into the box. The list might include:
- Tack and equipment for the show, including saddle and bridle, riding hats, clothing, crops, numbers and string with which to attach them, a spare set of clothes and protective overalls; tack cleaning kit for a final touch up, grooming kit and show sheen; summer sheet and sweat sheet, waterproof cover for the horse, fly repellent and plaiting kit; bucket, sponge and sweat scraper to wash the horse down with if he sweats up.

131

- Drinking water and bucket for the horse as the water at the show may not be plentiful or suitable. Haynet, bucket and a small amount of feed for the horse may be useful for tempting a shy loader.
- Loading equipment close to hand, including lunge reins, lunge whip and loading devices. Any loading equipment which is used should be packed in the horsebox in case it is required for the return journey.
- Spare string for emergencies.
- A spare set of pre-rolled bandages is useful, as owners may not have had time to roll up the set previously used.
- A first aid kit for both horse and human, including the basic first aid equipment and the vet's telephone number (*see* Chapter 6).
- Maps for the journey and contact number of the organizers.
- Money and food for humans.
- All equipment should be checked to ensure that it is safe prior to the journey. For example, leathers on a show saddle that haven't been used for a season may start to rot, or old travelling bandages may have lost their tying-up strings.
- It may be useful to take a brick or block of wood on the journey in case the ground is uneven at the show. This will level the ramp so it does not bounce and scare the horse.
- The horse's travel clothing should be laid out ready to put on, so there is no fuss or searching for equipment when it is time to go.

## Travel Clothing

The amount of clothing the horse wears will largely depend on the time of year. Most shows are in the summer, when the horse could become over-heated with too many layers of clothing. The basic items of clothing are:

**Leg protection** Bandages and padding, or travelling boots are necessary. Boots are much easier to put on, especially if the horse fidgets, and with the longer versions they offer extra protection. For ultimate leg protection, both boots and bandages may be used.

**Boots** There are several kinds of boots available: the shorter transport boots which run from knee or hock joint to coronet, commonly used for short journeys; and longer travelling boots, running from coronary band to above the knee or hock joint and offering greater protection; and knee and hock boots, which also add protection.

**Bandages and padding** When applied to the leg, the gamgee or foam padding should just cover the coronary band, so the entire lower leg is protected from knocks. The covering bandages must not be so tight as to restrict movement, and not so loose they could come undone and the horse could tread on them. Hock and knee boots are available for added protection, and are particularly useful when using bandages or transport boots.

**Tail protection** This is necessary to prevent the tail from rubbing against the partition or ramp. Tail bandages are commonly used but time-consuming to administer; tubular bandages with applicators are much quicker and just as cheap. Tail bags will have the added bonus of keeping plaits in place, and protecting the base of the tail from stains.

**Leather headcollar** This must be breakable in the event of an accident and have a strong leadrope.

**Poll guard** To protect the horse's head should he rear.

**Travelling rug** This is necessary when the weather is colder or if the box or trailer is draughty. They can be any form of rug, from lightweight sweat rugs and summer sheets to heavy woollen rugs. Wicking rugs seem most useful, so if the horse sweats, the moisture is taken away from the skin and the heat is retained. Owners who do not compete all year round may not need a special travelling rug, as they are usually used in cold weather. A thin sheet or stable rug will be just as suitable.

## Loading the Horse

Horses that have been taught to load from an early age are often no trouble and walk up the

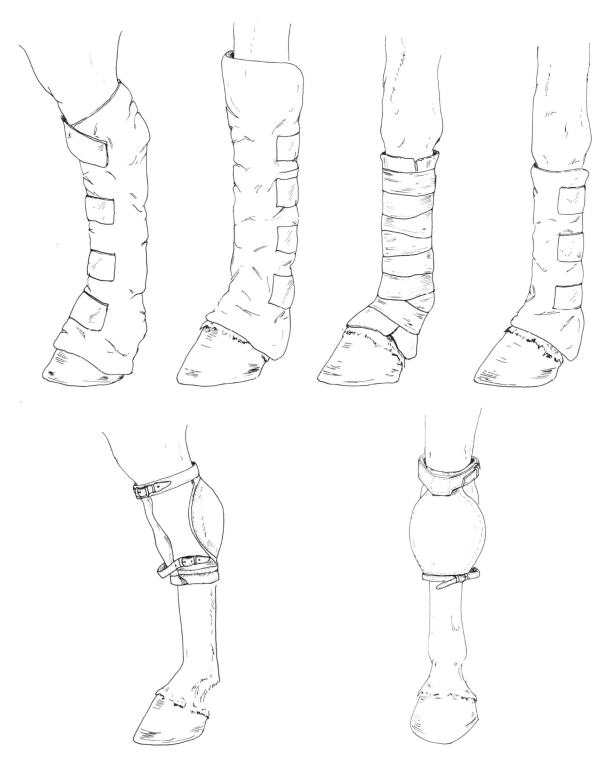

*Travelling boots.*

*Some horses are not good loaders, and it may take plenty of time, patience and practice before they become confident.*

ramp calmly and obediently. Others are less predictable and may take hours of patient cajoling before they overcome their seemingly irrational fear, which may have been caused by a previous bad experience. Others are simply pig-headed, not in the least bit frightened and just being disobedient!

Firstly when loading, the handler and assistants should be wearing protective hat and gloves. It is useful to park the horsebox or

*When loading, the horse should be led firmly up the centre of the ramp.*

trailer next to a wall or hedge so the horse cannot swing out to one side, and any hazards should be removed, such as the yard gate being firmly shut in case the horse breaks free. If there is a front ramp it may be helpful to lower it, to allow more light into the area. The horse will be happier if he knows the small space is not so confined. The same goes for windows and groom's doors, anything to let in extra light. The ramp should have a non-slip surface, like rubber matting or a sprinkling of shavings or straw. Partitions may be moved over so the horse has a wider space to walk into, though seasoned loaders may not need this precaution. When travelling one horse in a trailer, he should travel on the right-hand side. This will balance the trailer and make for a more comfortable journey, as the vehicle will naturally slant to the left due to the camber of the road.

A headcollar may be suitable for obedient horses, but a bridle will give the handler a little more control. Leading with a lunge rein will also allow more control in the event of the horse pulling back and trying to escape. The handler should walk as much as possible at the shoulder so they are not pulling the horse, making sure the horse walks in straight. If he comes in at an angle, he may slip off the ramp. It is important to be firm at all times, and not turn round and look at the horse. A bowl of feed in one hand will encourage the horse to walk in, allowing him to stop and have a mouthful each time he makes a few steps. An encouraging tone will also help, though for the pig-headed horse an authoritative one may be more useful! It is never any use losing one's temper, so it is always important handlers stay calm, as the horse will sense the tense atmosphere. As soon as the horse has walked into the box or trailer, the assistant should quickly put the partition in place and attach the breeching strap behind the horse's rump before putting up the ramp. This must never be put up before the strap because if the horse panics, he may try to reverse, bringing the ramp down on top of the handler. More difficult horses may

require assistance from behind. Two lunge reins attached to each side of the trailer or box and gradually crossed behind the horse's rump may encourage him forward, but must be done carefully lest he panics. Loading devices work on a similar premise. Some are in the form of plastic banners which when held beneath the horse's rump by two assistants encourage him forward. However, they must stand well clear of the back legs in case the horse should kick out. As some loading assistants may be non-horsey friends or family of the competitor, it is useful if they are given a grounding on safety and the horse's likely reactions before loading. They may not be quick enough to see a kick coming if they have little experience around

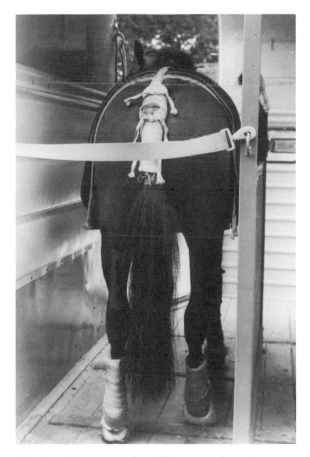

*The breeching strap should be secured in place before the ramp is lifted.*

horses. Once the horse is safely inside, he should be tied on a reasonably short rope to a piece of breakable twine around a ring, and given a haynet to keep him occupied. Though handlers may stay with the horse in a horse-box along the journey to calm him down, this is not allowed in a trailer and is dangerous.

The driving should always be done by a knowledgeable person, particularly in the case of pulling trailers. Drivers should practice several times before taking the horse on board to get the feel of the additional weight, especially when reversing, which is always difficult for first time trailer-pullers. Anyone with a full driving licence obtained before

> **ECONOMIZE**
>
> - Instead of buying a poll guard, wrap a spare bandage around the top of the travelling headcollar, making sure there is extra padding over the poll.
> - Take a spare set of everything to a show. In the event of loss or damage, buying some more equipment at the show is much more expensive.
> - A fillet string can be made to secure a rug used for travelling, by plaiting together three pieces of cord or bailer twine, then stitching loosely to the rug.

1996 can pull a trailer, though a new law is being introduced whereby a test must be taken by new drivers wishing to pull trailers. Likewise if the horsebox is classed as a heavy goods vehicle, drivers will need to take an additional HGV test.

When unloading from a trailer with only one ramp, it should be lowered once the horse is untied, and the breeching strap left until last. It is best if the horse reverses slowly and carefully down the ramp, though he should be left to his own devices and not be held back or pulled by the handler. If he is able to walk forwards down the ramp in the case of front unloading trailers or horseboxes, this will be more desirable as he will be able to see where he is going. Again, handlers should let the horse sort himself out, as interference may cause him to trip.

It is always best to allow plenty of time for loading and travelling, just in case the horse is a problem to load. It is better to arrive at the show with time to spare rather than dashing around and missing the class.

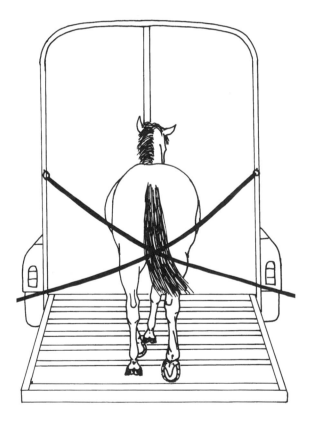

*Two crossed lunge reins may encourage the horse forward.*

# 9 Safety and Security

## SAFETY AND SECURITY

There are many things responsible horse owners must do to keep their horses, equipment and property unharmed. Having previously discussed yard safety, routine safety checks around the yard and tack inspection, this section looks at additional safety procedures and security measures owners can take.

### Fire Precautions

This has to be one of the most important areas of hazard prevention. Just one small spark can send an entire yard up in flames, destroying everything and endangering equine and human life into the bargain. There are several basic points that when followed may prevent the onset of fire:

- No smoking anywhere on the yard. There may be many highly flammable objects around the yard, such as wooden stables and stacks of hay or straw. 'No Smoking' signs should be prominently displayed, even if the yard is private with few visitors.
- The muck heap must not be situated too close to buildings, particularly if it is managed by burning.
- Hay and straw stacks are a fire hazard, particularly if they are deep and could get very hot. Spontaneous combustion of hay and straw does happen (and I can verify this from personal experience), so all owners should be aware of the possibility.
- There must be at least one red $CO_2$ fire extinguisher at the yard, though a green foam filled and blue powder filled extinguisher in addition is advisable. These must

be checked twice a year by the local fire officer to ensure they are in good working order.
- A smoke alarm will also be a very good investment.
- If there is more than one person present at the yard there must be a fire drill that everyone is familiar with. The usual procedure

*Safety checks on all wiring, electrical equipment and yard facilities should be made regularly.*

137

is: Raise the alarm then turn the horses out in to a safe field and telephone the fire brigade. As some stables are quite remote it may be useful to send someone to meet them at the driveway. Tackle the fire if possible. It is important to stay calm, particularly as the horses may be panicking. It is always advised that human life must come before equine, no matter how desperate the situation.

- There should be a fire hose at all commercial yards, though some private yards may not be this well equipped.
- All wiring should be regularly checked and maintained, particularly in older buildings. Keeping vermin down is a form of fire prevention, as they may chew through electricity cables and inadvertently cause a fire.
- Fire buckets filled with sand should be positioned throughout the yard, and maintained.
- The local fire officer will go through the fire procedure and assess the amount of fire hazards present at the yard when he checks the extinguishers. His advice should be followed as it may save lives.

## Riding and Road Safety

Anyone who rides horses outside of their own property should have a rudimentary knowledge of road safety. In fact it is their duty to do so, as accidents caused by thoughtless riders may affect others, and will give conscientious riders a bad name. It is a very sad fact that in Great Britain there are around sixteen riders killed every year, and an astounding eight horse-related accidents on the road daily (3,000 annually).

The British Horse Society suggests that 'all riders should be aware of their own position and that of all other road users, with courtesy, safety and conspicuity being equally important.' This includes thanking other road users for slowing down and wearing reflective clothing all the time. Though at dusk the clothing is invaluable, throughout the day it is also advised, as drivers will be able to see riders

from a greater distance. Reflective clothing for riders includes tabards, hat silks, arm bands and gloves, and for the horse, exercise sheets, boots, leg wraps and bridle wear.

It is recommended that the BHS Riding and Road Safety Test is taken by all riders. Applicants must be able to ride independently at walk, trot and canter, and be between the ages of twelve and seventy.

## Security

Unfortunately horse and equipment theft is on the increase, with thieves going to any lengths to obtain the goods. There are several precautions owners can take, as without their vigilance the thieves' job is made easier.

The theft of the horse itself can be discouraged to a certain degree and one of the most reliable methods is freezemarking. There are several companies that carry out the service, and they come out to the yard to brand the horse with a security number that is recorded at a central database. This is as individual as a car number plate, and is usually marked on the horse's back on one side of the spine, though in some cases may it may be on the shoulder. On dark-skinned horses, the number is seen as white hair, though due to their skin pigmentation, on light-coloured horses the number is seen as bald skin. Light coloured horses will need the freezemarked area clipped in the winter, as the long hair may cover up the mark. The process is painless as well as providing the authorities with a means of identifying the horse, and also acting as a deterrent to potential thieves. Signs for display around the yard and badges to sew on rugs are available, and might make thieves think twice. Though some years ago there was talk of freezemarked horses being discriminated against in the show ring, this theory holds no ground now. After all, any safety-conscious judge will have had their own horses freezemarked!

Another method is to brand the horse's feet with the owner's postcode. Branding irons are available to owners from some equine

*Freeze-marking or security branding will provide owners with peace of mind.*

security companies for the farrier's use, though some recommended farriers offer the service for around the same price as a trim. In addition, signs are provided for display around the yard and field, acting as a further deterrent for thieves.

Owners should also take photographs of their horses from all angles, and of any markings or scars that may help in the identification process.

Most horses are stolen from their fields, as there is often no one present at all times to keep watch. Thieves may monitor the owners so they know when they are out and the horses are unsupervised. A thick hedge makes an excellent deterrent for thieves. They are unlikely to spend time trying to break through it, and the horse will not be keen to walk through a gap. Wire fencing is the easiest to break through, though wooden or synthetic fences pose little problem for well equipped thieves. All gates should be padlocked at both sides so they can not be lifted off their hinges, and the horse's headcollar may be left off so he is less easy to catch.

Yard gates should also be padlocked at both ends, and if possible the yard should be alarmed. Alarms are the best method of deterring thieves from yards, preferably combined with security lights. Though some systems may be expensive, it is well worth the effort in the long run. Guard dogs are an excellent deterrent. Those specifically trained for the purpose and not kept as pets will not let anyone strange in to the yard, and may act as an early warning of prowlers should they see or smell anyone different.

All storage and tack rooms should be locked and secured carefully, including window bars, after all it is just as easy for thieves to go through the window! Owners should check with their insurance companies with regard to theft of tack, as there may be specifications with regard to storage and what type of locks should be used.

For identification purposes, all tack and equipment should be marked with the owner's postcode or national insurance number. Security companies and some tack shops stock marking tools, which leave an indented mark on leather. Indelible security pens can also be used to mark tack unobtrusively, but for deterrent purposes, rugs and other equipment can be marked with fluorescent or bright paint — anything to render the equipment less sellable! Owners should check that the paint will not dissolve stitching or damage the equipment.

Several security companies offer a trailer marking service which is similar to freeze-marking. The number is stored on a database and is put on the sides and roof of the trailer with strong adhesive vinyl. Signs can also be prominently displayed in the vicinity to deter thieves.

# THE LAW

Many of the legal problems horse owners face involve agreements, whether they be legal contracts or verbal. The majority of agreements are not legal, for instance, with the owner who rents land or stables, or pays livery without receiving receipts. In the event of accidents or cases of negligence, it could come down to one word against the other. It is therefore preferable to have some kind of written, signed agreement if at all possible, though some land owners, fully aware of the accident prone and inquisitive nature of horses, may not be keen to sign.

## Renting Grazing

As previously stated, if at all possible, a written agreement should be drawn up and signed, and a copy reserved by both parties. It should include the date of agreement and expiry, and the names and details of the land owner and person renting stated. Details, such as the number of horses grazing on the land and amount of money being paid, should also be listed, and a statement from each party regarding their obligations. For instance, an agreement should be made between the land owner who maintains the condition of the field and fencing, and the person renting, honestly stating the horse is not destructive or diseased. An agreement of compensation on the land owner's part and terms of notice for the agreement should also be listed, and the contract signed by both parties and two witnesses.

In the event of a contract not being made, the person renting must rely on their legal right to rent land on which the horse can enjoy quiet enjoyment. The land must remain in the same condition as when it was first rented, which includes a safe environment free from hazards (assuming the person renting was satisfied the land was safe in the first place). A letter of thanks could be written from the person renting to the land owner, including an informal statement of what the tenant understands both parties' rights and terms to be. Though it would not be a legal document, it would put the land owner in a position to object or agree to the rights and terms.

## Renting Stabling

The tenant's rights run along similar lines when renting stabling. A written contract is desirable including the same details as previously mentioned, though may not be agreed to by the yard owner. However, when renting stables and offering facilities, the yard owner may want an agreement with regard to the tenant's obligations, as the yard owner would have more potential risks at a yard than in a field. For instance, the horse owner could fall off while riding in the school and injure himself on a jump wing, or have tack stolen from the tack room. The yard owner would not want to risk getting sued in such cases and may want to draw up a contract to state liability in these circumstances. Some yard owners will display a disclaimer notice with regard to liability, though these are not actually legal agreements.

Without a signed contract, tenants are in the same position as when renting land, in that the yard owner must provide a safe environment consistent with the condition it was in when the tenant agreed to rent. The informal letter may again be useful, as the yard owner would have been given the opportunity to agree or disagree with the terms laid out. It is in the owner's interests to find out what insurance cover the yard owners have with regard to injury or death, and take out their own insurance for themselves and most importantly the horse.

## Insurance

Individuals are urged to take out insurance against third part liability and death or injury to themselves and their horses. The horse's cover may include accident or injury, death from any cause, theft, accidents involving third parties, and theft of tack or equipment (such as trailers or carts).

It is a legal obligation of the horse owner to make sure the animal does not stray. For instance, if the horse got out of his field and damaged someone's garden or caused an accident, the owner would be liable, and the situation quite cut and dried. However, liability with regard to riding accidents, where another party is injured encompasses a minefield of considerations. To simplify the rationale, in order for the rider to be at fault he must be negligent. However, errors of judgement and circumstances beyond the rider's control do not necessarily mean negligence, and this goes for the other party (for instance a car driver) as well. It is to do with what is expected, that is the rider on public roads is expected to be capable and in control of his mount, and the driver is expected to slow down and approach a horse with caution. However, the

─── ECONOMIZE ───

The only form of economy owners can make as far as safety and security are concerned is a long-term one. That is to make sure any thefts are prevented at all costs; marking and securing all equipment deters any thieves.

owner of the horse is legally liable for accident or damage caused to another party unless they (the other party) or someone else admits responsibility, or in the judge's opinion there were mitigating circumstances.

One word of warning for owners: read the small print of insurance policies, as loopholes may render the cover void. Examples include the type of bolt used to secure equipment, or the necessity for safety helmets and vaccinations. The conditions of pay-out vary enormously, so it is down to the person taking out the insurance to read and understand the agreement and the general conditions.

*Unfortunately, horse theft is common, so owners must take the relevant precautions to ensure that their yards are secure.*

# Index ———————————————————————